SHIPWRECKS
of the
OUTER BANKS

DRAMATIC RESCUES AND FANTASTIC WRECKS IN THE GRAVEYARD OF THE ATLANTIC

JAMES D. CHARLET

Globe
Pequot

Guilford, Connecticut

Globe
Pequot

An imprint of The Rowman & Littlefield Publishing Group, Inc.
4501 Forbes Blvd., Ste. 200
Lanham, MD 20706
www.rowman.com

Distributed by NATIONAL BOOK NETWORK

British Library Cataloguing in Publication Information available
Library of Congress Control Number: 2019953936

ISBN 978-1-4930- 3590-8 (hardback)
ISBN 978-1-4930-3589-2 (e-book)

To Sumner Increase Kimball,
Superintendent United States Life-Saving Service
Due to "The Single Most Important Shipwreck in American History"—
see Chapter 20, Section "The Phoenix Arises."

And to Mom,
Who said "You're a writer, son" since I was a child.

CONTENTS

PREFACE

Call me Keeper James. My baptism by fire started with becoming the keeper of the Chicamacomico Life-Saving Station Historic Site and Museum in the quaint village of Rodanthe, on the iconic Cape Hatteras, the island centerpiece of North Carolina's fabled Outer Banks. That, in turn, ignited a passion for the unique history of the United States Life-Saving Service, which eventually led to me becoming keeper of Outer Banks history, geography, and culture. This book is a spark of that enlightenment and passion.

I.

THE BIG PICTURE

CHAPTER 1

THE US LIFE-SAVING SERVICE ON THE OUTER BANKS

From 1871 to 1915, almost three hundred USLSS stations dotted America's coastlines. The surfmen of these stations had the singular mission of saving lives in peril from the sea. During their forty-four-year history nationwide, these brave souls responded to more than 178,000 such lives in peril, of which they saved over 177,000 . . . yet somehow, America has forgotten these peaceful heroes.

The Beginning

The very first lifesavers on the Outer Banks were the original European settlers. They were severely isolated and lived an extremely difficult, hardscrabble life. Their very existence was dependent upon helping each other, so it was only natural when a shipwreck occurred within their sight that they would go to help. No records were kept of these activities, so we have no hard data. But these were clearly the first Outer Banks volunteer lifesavers.

It continued that way for decades. It wasn't until 1874 that what were to become the first United States Coast Guard stations on the Outer

START OF THE SERVICE

The term **United States Life-Saving Service** first appeared officially in the *Congressional Record* in 1848 when a New Jersey congressman sponsored a bill referring to a few stations along New Jersey and
Long Island to protect the New York harbor, the Unites States' busiest
port. Most historians recognize that the Service began nationally in 1871.

Banks were derived from a federal organization called the United States
Life-Saving Service (USLSS).

The USLSS, sometimes called simply "the Service," existed nationally
on all of America's coasts, including the Great Lakes, from 1871 to
1915, when it merged with the US Revenue Cutter Service to become
the US Coast Guard. The US Life-Saving Service had a singular mission: to save lives in peril from the sea.

The British had established a national lifesaving service in 1824,
called the Royal National Lifeboat Institution (RNLI). Despite its
name, it was entirely staffed with volunteers and funded totally by
public contributions. Remarkably, it remains that way today. By the
time America got around to implementing a national lifesaving service,
the RNLI was a highly successful fine-tuned machine offering a useful
blueprint for Americans to follow.

An article from the British *Lifeboat Magazine Archive*, dated 1880, is
a gold mine of primary source information. Keep in mind that this was
published merely nine years after our US Life-Saving Service was fully
established.

Life-Boats and Life-Saving Apparatus in the United States of America

We have in previous numbers of the *Life-boat Journal* given
accounts of the Life-saving [*sic*] Institutions of France and
Germany and have referred to those in other maritime countries

of Europe. We feel sure that equal interest will be felt in a description of the means provided for the protection of human life from ship-wrecks on the shores of that land, first peopled by Englishmen, the greatness and prosperity of which, born of British energy, enterprise, and love of liberty, ought to afford us the same pride and satisfaction that is felt by a parent in the progress and success of a son, even if in course of time it should eclipse his own. . . .

"God speed," and expressing the earnest hope that the only rivalry between the two great nations in the future ages may be the noble one of endeavouring [*sic*] to excel in every humane and good work for the happiness and welfare of our respective countries and the good of mankind.[1]

The first Outer Banks Life-Saving Service (LSS) stations were built and manned in 1874. They were, from north to south, Jones Hill (then Whale Head, and later, with the more-familiar name "Currituck Beach"), Caffeys Inlet, Kitty Hawk, Nags Head, Bodie Island (renamed "Oregon Inlet"), Chicamacomico (now, the village of Rodanthe), and Little Kinnakeet (just north of today's village of Avon). In 1878, eleven more stations were added. These included the now-famous Kill Devil Hills station, which assisted the Wright brothers (see chapter 15), and the Hatteras Inlet Station. Still more were added by century's end, eventually totaling twenty-nine, averaging about six miles apart on the North Carolina outer coast from the Virginia line (Wash Woods LSS–1878), to the South Carolina line (Oak Island LSS–1886). In 1915, all of these became Coast Guard stations.

US Life-Saving Service Stations, 1871–1915: The Basics

Eventually, nearly three hundred stations were located on all of America's coasts: Atlantic, Pacific, Great Lakes, and even a few on the Gulf Coast. Although the architecture of the stations changed greatly over the years and they varied between regions, routines were consistent.

REGULATIONS FOR THE GOVERNMENT OF THE LIFE-SAVING SERVICE OF THE UNITED STATES, 1899[2]

Contents

I. Appointment and qualifications of officers and crew

II. Duties of officers and crew

III. Absence from duty

IV. Patrol

V. Drill and exercise

VI. Action at wrecks

VII. Uniform

VIII. General provisions to be observed by officers and crew

IX. Telephone service

All stations were governed by a strict set of highly specific and detailed rules and regulations contained in a five-and-a-half-by-nine-inch, roughly 200-page manual entitled *Regulations for the Government of the Life-Saving Service of the United States*, issued to every station and updated every year. The men just called it "the Book."

Drills and Duties

Every station in the country did the same routine every day of the week: On Monday they practiced the beach apparatus drill; Tuesday, the surfboat drill; Wednesday, flag-signaling practice; Thursday was a repeat of the beach apparatus drill, showing its importance; Friday, they learned and practiced first aid; Saturdays were used for cleaning (and repairing, if needed) the station and equipment, as well as themselves and their tools and clothes. Sunday was a day off, but they were still on call, since the surfmen lived nearby, within earshot of the station's bell.

By 1878, in addition to these daily drills, every surfman had two vital duties: keeping the watch, and beach patrol.

The beaches were covered twenty-four hours a day, seven days a week—a monumental task. If a shipwreck occurred, a station would know about it within minutes. It might take them hours to get there, but they knew of it and took action immediately. How did they do this? Every station had a watchtower, usually a separate tower on the highest level above the roof. These were manned from sunup to sundown. The stations in North Carolina eventually averaged about six to seven miles apart. The watchman on one tower could see his neighboring stations to the north and the south. This obviously did not work at night or on days with visibility obscured by fog, rain, or storms.

Then it was time for the beach patrol. Two men from each station were sent to the beach all at the same time. According to Superintendent Sumner Kimball himself, "The night patrol was divided into four watches—one from sunset to 8 o'clock, one from 8 to 12, one from 12 to 4, and one from 4 to sunrise."[3] They would walk in opposite directions, heading toward their neighboring station. They would meet the neighboring station's surfman on beach patrol halfway, chat, and exchange beach checks to prove to their keeper that the patrol was complete.

They not only looked for recent shipwrecks but also for potential shipwrecks. If they spotted a shipwreck, the surfman would send up a flare to notify the station of the wreck, and the shipwrecked crew that they had been spotted. The flare encouraged the crew to remain on the ship. The primary cause of death and injury in shipwrecks was from jumping into the water and then being hit by huge chunks of debris or drowning. Importantly, the flare announced that professional help was on the way. As soon as the station crew saw the flare, they set out to help immediately.

The surfman would also send up a flare if they spotted a ship too close to the visible shore or the invisible shoals below to warn "Alter course away from here!" They also carried lanterns to light their way.

Each surfman in the Service was issued an exclusive identification tag, called a beach check. Every beach check in the entire Service bore a unique combination of three numbers: the district (of thirteen) in the United States, the station within that district, and the individual surfman number (1–8) within that station. This is why they exchanged beach checks on patrol: to prove completion of their patrol.

The Lifesaving Equipment

Every station had identical equipment which made for smooth transfers from one station to another. The US Coast Guard continues this same technique today, which partly accounts for their incredible efficiency. According to Superintendent Kimball, the stations (other than the houses of refuge) were generally equipped with two surfboats (supplied with oars, lifeboat compass, and other outfits), a boat carriage, two sets of breeches-buoy apparatus (including a Lyle gun and accessories), a cart for the transportation of the apparatus, a life car, twenty cork jackets, two heaving sticks, a dozen Coston signals, a dozen signal rockets, a set of signal flags of the International Code, a medicine chest with contents, a barometer, a thermometer, patrol lanterns, patrol checks or patrol clocks, the requisite furniture for rude housekeeping by the crew and for the succor of rescued people, fuel and oil, tools for the repair of the boats and apparatus and for minor repairs to the buildings, and the necessary books and stationery. To facilitate the transportation of boats and apparatus to scenes of shipwrecks, a pair of horses was also provided at stations where they could not be hired, and to those stations where the supplies, mails, etc., had to be brought by water, a supply boat was furnished.[4]

Each station had two basic types of boats: **lifeboats** or **surfboats**. Most used one or the other; a few had both. Both were row- and sail-powered in the beginning and later converted to motor power. Lifeboats were larger and used for rough waters. They could be launched on rails from the station. Surfboats, on the other hand, were designed specifically for calmer waters where they were launched, as in North

Carolina. They were smaller, sleeker, and more maneuverable. They had no transom, meaning the bow and stern were the same pointed shape in case they got turned around. The Beebe-McLellan was the most common surfboat in the Outer Banks stations. Today's Coast Guard still designates nineteen special stations as surf stations. Only four of those are on the East Coast, and Hatteras Island has two of them: Motor Lifeboat Stations (MLB) Oregon Inlet and Hatteras Inlet.

The **beach apparatus** was the collective term for the beach cart loaded with all of its individual pieces. This was the preferred means of rescue for two reasons: If there were hundred-mile-per-hour winds, thirty-foot seas, and stinging rain, the last thing you wanted to do was put another boat in the water. Secondly, the surfmen could remain more safely on the beach.

The Lyle gun was the most striking. It was a small, bronze, 200-pound black-powder mortar designed specifically for this purpose, with the unique distinction of being the only gun in the history of humankind specifically designed to save, and not take, lives. Its muzzle would be loaded with a twenty-pound steel projectile called the shot. Attached to the shot was a long but thin line of hemp rope, called the shot line. This line was woven between tall wooden pins in a large box called the shot box, or the "faking" box. It was dumped out before firing. This kept the line from fouling or tangling as it exited the gun at great speed.

Two large drums or reels were high on the front of the cart. They carried the whip lines. Although they looked like two separate lines, it was actually one long line running through a central pulley, or "block," to the mariners. In the actual rescue, the objective was to fire the projectile over the ship so that the shot line fell in the ship's rigging. Someone aboard the ship—crewman (or passenger, if necessary)—would then retrieve that line and begin to haul it in. Tied to the end of it was the whip line. When the pulley reached the ship, it was tied high up on a mast. The two ends remained on the whip line and were spread in a *V* shape.

Now, by attaching something to one whip line and pulling on the other, that item would go out to the ship. Reversing it, naturally, would bring it back to shore from the ship—picture Grandma's old clothesline.

The first thing to be tied to a whip line was the hawser. This was a large, heavy, thick line stored in the bottom of the cart. It was hauled out to the ship and secured just above the whip-line block. Meanwhile, two surfmen would have been digging an *X*-shaped hole on the beach, three to four feet deep. Into this excavation was placed the sand anchor, two large flat boards in that shape with a ring to which a line could be attached. It was then buried, and the shore end of the hawser attached to it. The hawser was tightened by most of the surfmen using the fall line, a series of pulleys that multiplied the pulling force.

The breeches buoy was then attached to one of the whip lines. Finally, the crotch pole was inserted under the hawser to gain even more height and tension. Now the breeches buoy could be hauled off to the ship by manning one whip line, loading one survivor, and bringing them safely ashore by hauling off the other whip line. This process was so effective that its last use by the Coast Guard was in 1962.

How did ships' crews know what to do with this somewhat complicated procedure? First, a tally board was sent out with the hawser with brief written instructions. Insurance companies had a vested interest in reducing the loss of lives and cargo, so they printed a more

Layout of the Beach Apparatus Drill, photo of page 103 of author's copy of the 1899 Regulations for the Governance of the Life-Saving Service of the United States. *Author's Photo*

comprehensive booklet entitled "Instructions to Mariners in Case of Shipwreck," with text and illustrations. These were required to be on board any insured vessel, and they did help save lives.

Every station had at least two beach carts. One was the drill cart, which carried one of everything, since this was only used at the station for the Monday and Thursday practices. The wreck cart was much larger and heavier. Since they might have been miles from the station and caught in bad weather, which usually was the case, this cart carried six steel shots, three faked shot boxes and extra powder, lines and rope, plus additional tools.

Finally, each station was furnished with a **life car**. This was a small metal car that resembled a submarine and could carry seven prone survivors. It would be used in place of the breeches buoy. This was one of those good ideas that didn't always work and quickly fell into disuse.

The Life-Saving Service Did It All

The nationwide stations of the US Life-Saving Service routinely went above and beyond their regimented schedule and demands. In addition to the daily drills, daily duties, and actual rescues, the Service did much more. When survivors were brought back to the station, they were immediately given first aid that the men were trained in every Friday. Quickly they were given dry clothing, food, water, and succor. They were given a place to stay until arrangements could be made by the shipping company to pick them up. All of this was free of charge. (The station would contact the shipping company and notify them of the wreck and the situation.) The surfmen offered to unload salvageable cargo if practical. If not, the men would often stand by the wrecked ship for days at a time to prevent scavenging. The surfmen buried the people that did not survive. The last thing the keeper would do was write a detailed wreck report. They did it all. And this didn't take into consideration all the things they did for their villagers.

In North Carolina, most of these lifesaving stations were in very remote places that were difficult to access. Villages typically grew around stations if they weren't built in or near an existing small fishing settlement. These villages typically contained no more than several hundred people. The families were largely related to each other. Each Outer Banks village had a predominant family name: Scarborough, Gray, O'Neal, Hooper, Burrus, Daniels, Etheridge, Jennett, Fulchur, and Midgett, among others. Oddly, these villages were highly competitive with each other.

Nevertheless, the Life-Saving Station in each became the center of that village in several ways. Because they had the only connections to the outside world—first telegraph, then radio, and finally telephone—they became the communication center of the village. The Chicamacomico Station, for example, merely thirty-six miles from Kitty Hawk, heard about the Wright brothers' success in 1903 (see chapter 15) at their station in Rodanthe. Villagers could also communicate their news—weddings, births, anniversaries, deaths—to relatives this way.

Since these men were trained weekly in first aid, the station also became the "urgent care center" of the village. The men of the Service had become national heroes through constant coverage in newspapers and magazines of the times. They wore uniforms, had medals and ribbons, and held coveted and highly respected jobs.

Everybody loves a hero, so these stations also became social centers, since villagers naturally congregated there. They also became the village welcome center and chamber of commerce for visitors just passing through. The stations interacted with their villagers and offered help any way they could, since the lifesavers were usually related to most of the population of that village!

What Is Left

Very little of these original stations remain. Caffeys Inlet LSS Station has been converted to the Lifesaving Restaurant, part of the Sanderling Resort in the Outer Banks town of Duck. Nearly unrecognizable today, it has been extremely modified and modernized. The Kitty Hawk station was similarly converted to the Black Pelican Restaurant.

Unless you know what to look for, its origins can easily be missed. The Kill Devil Hills station has become the office of the Twiddy Insurance Company and moved to Corolla. The 1898 Oregon Inlet Station is a restored but abandoned structure seen while crossing the 2019 Marc Basnight Bridge (locally known as the Oregon Inlet Bridge), the first building oceanside on Hatteras Island.

Chicamacomico LSS Station is the only fully restored North Carolina station, now a museum open to the public. One of the other five remaining stations built in the 1911 Chicamacomico style is a beach rental cottage in Kill Devil Hills, again, highly modernized, but still very recognizable. Little Kinnakeet had its 1874 station beautifully reconstructed, and its 1904 station exists, but at this writing is badly in need of restoration. Owned by the National Park Service, neither is currently open to the public. Just south of that is Creeds Hill. This 1918 Chatham-type station is a private "beach getaway" not open to the public. Portsmouth Station, even farther south on Portsmouth Island, has been beautifully and expertly restored by the National Park Service. This one *is* open to the public, but it is challenging to get to, being accessible only by boat.

The 1888 Cape Lookout Station exists, but not for much longer at the current rate of decay. It is unrestored, unrepaired, unattended, and has seriously deteriorated over the years. The 1889 Oak Island LSS station has been beautifully restored, but with a modern interior, as it is now a private residence. West and south of Wilmington, it was the southernmost of all North Carolina Life-Saving Stations.

Thus, twelve of the original twenty-nine stations exist in some form or another. The other seventeen are completely gone. Some were destroyed by storms; some simply fell apart over the years due to abandonment; and some were destroyed purposely after being decommissioned.

Yet the architectural legacy remains. Throughout the Outer Banks today, architectural clues from old Life-Saving Stations abound in houses and businesses, chiefly from the distinctive style of 1874–1878 and the 1880s. The most common are representations of the watchtower, or roof pitch decoration. Once you know what to look for, these motifs are easy to spot, and you will find them everywhere!

Today's Modern Outer Banks US Coast Guard Stations

The modern Outer Banks USCG stations include US Coast Guard Motor Lifeboat Station Oregon Inlet, MLB Station Hatteras Inlet, and Aids to Navigation (ANT) Station Wanchese. There are more stations on the remainder of the North Carolina coast, but these are the ones along the Outer Banks. Another USCG station located near the Outer Banks is Air Station Elizabeth City (ASEC). Only ninety minutes' drive (seventy-two miles) from Oregon Inlet, USCG-ASEC is the second-largest Coast Guard Air Station in America. It serves the entire Atlantic Coast and is often deployed elsewhere (and is the hero of chapter 7).

Life-Saving Stations were originally placed as close together as possible in order to cover the entire coast. Everything was done manually. They had to haul the boats and the beach carts by manpower. They had to patrol the beaches on foot. But by the mid-1950s, all that had changed drastically. High-powered surfboats that were self-righting and self-bailing could be on scene much more quickly than before, and they didn't have to be so close to the ocean, in the way of harmful storms. Russian-American Igor Sikorsky had invented an incredible flying machine that was perfect for maritime rescues: the helicopter. In 1954, Lockheed-Martin had invented the C-130 "Hercules" cargo plane, perfect for long-distance rescue support. In that same year, NC Highway 12 was first completed and opened to traffic on Hatteras Island, Bodie Island, and Ocracoke Island, again increasing transit speed.

Consequently, fewer stations were needed, and they could be farther apart and farther inland. That is why they are located where they are today.

Coast Guard Motor Lifeboat Station Hatteras Inlet is located on the southern end of Hatteras Island, North Carolina, adjacent to the Hatteras ferry docks. The unit's building was constructed on six acres of National Park Service land. The station is equipped with two forty-seven-foot surfboats (the kind designed to sustain a rollover in heavy seas) and other rescue facilities. Station Hatteras Inlet also covers Ocracoke Island during the summer.

As a multi-mission unit, Station Hatteras Inlet conducts search and rescue (SAR), boating safety, law enforcement, and marine environmental protection operations. There is a boat crew available twenty-four hours a day that responds to more than 150 calls for assistance annually. The station's Area of Responsibility (AOR) includes more than 2,350 square nautical miles of the Atlantic Ocean, one-third of the Pamlico Sound, and half of Ocracoke Island. This area includes Diamond Shoals, also known as the "Graveyard of the Atlantic." Of all those missions, search and rescue is the most prominent. (You can follow them on Facebook.)

The origin of the name "Station Oregon Inlet" is shrouded. The name first appeared for a station near the inlet in 1874 as a US Life-Saving Service station, but named Bodie Island Station. It was located on the south side of the inlet. In 1883, the station on the north side of the inlet, "Tommy's Hummock," was renamed "Bodie Island Station." At the same time, the original Bodie Island Station, still located on the south side, was renamed "Oregon Inlet Station." In 1888 it was moved farther westward, but still on the south side. Less than a decade later, it was totally destroyed by a storm. A new station was built there and became operational in 1898. It was abandoned in 1988; the current station, now back on the north side, opened in 1990.

As a multi-mission unit, Station Oregon Inlet has the same missions as Hatteras Inlet. Their response to SARs is about two hundred a year. (You can follow them on Facebook as well.)

US Coast Guard Air Station Elizabeth City is *not* located on the Outer Banks, but it has a very distinct presence here. According to a public affairs officer at the Air Station, "Our bread and butter is SAR. We have H-60 and HC-130 crews in a B-0 status (meaning thirty minutes from call-out to takeoff) 24/7/365." Visitors to the Outer Banks will see these aircraft flying over frequently.

Probably one of the easiest things to overlook, or not even notice, are all the aids to navigation in the waters of the Outer Banks. There are literally hundreds of these buoys, channel markers, and lights that give vital information to mariners. Every one of these is placed, maintained, checked on, and repositioned as conditions change by Coast Guard Station ANT (Aids to Navigation) Wanchese as well as ANT Fort Macon and ANT Oak Island.

An Excellent Summary

Ralph Shank's book, *The US Life-Saving Service: Heroes, Rescues and Architecture of the Early Coast Guard*, is regarded by most maritime historians as one of the most authoritative sources on the subject. The opening paragraph of his book says it all: "They were the greatest heroes of the American coast, routinely risking their lives in the grand maritime rescues. Their work was respected and honored by America's most prestigious leaders, celebrated in the most popular publications of their time and of deep interest to medical, educational, religious, and political leaders. The Wright brothers knew them well, poet Walt Whitman wrote of them, and the artist Winslow Homer painted them. But somehow America forgot these peaceful heroes. Yet anyone reading of their bravery today will always remember them. The Life-Saving Service answered that most basic of human questions, 'Who will help in our hour of greatest need?'"[5]

In the forty-four years of the US Life-Saving Service, nation-wide, under the most adverse and dangerous conditions, these heroes responded to more than 178,000 lives in peril from the sea, *of which they saved over 177,000!* It bears repeating; somehow, America has forgotten these peaceful heroes.

Before the statistic is given for their own loss of life while engaging in these dreadfully dangerous rescues, consider the usual circumstances: storms producing massive waves the height of multistory buildings, winds strong enough to knock a human down, rain so hard there is little vision. They could respond to a wreck during a moonless night, a mosquito-infested scorching summer day, or a freezing winter day.

These brave surfmen, with cork life belts as their only safety equipment, did this time after time after time, to save complete strangers. Under these extreme conditions, their own loss of life on duty nationwide during these forty-four years was less than 1 percent.

In all the years I have talked about this remarkable history, I have made a stunning observation: Ninety-nine out of one hundred people have never even heard of the US Life-Saving Service—regardless of their age, level of education, residence, or worldly travel, *yet*, every one of them has heard of the Pony Express. That delivery service lasted only eighteen months and employed eighty-three teenage boys whose sole accomplishment was briefly riding a horse, fast. How can that be? Recording and remembering this history is a tribute to those peaceful heroes, lest America forget their sacrifice.

CHAPTER 2
WHY THE GRAVEYARD
OF THE ATLANTIC?

*The Atlantic Ocean covers 41,105,000 square miles, according to the
National Oceanic and Atmospheric Administration (NOAA). If we take the
"Graveyard of the Atlantic" to be the 300-mile coastline by twenty miles out
to sea, that amounts to only 0.0001459 percent of the entire ocean, yet it has
claimed five thousand ships. The common and obvious question—"Why were
there so many shipwrecks there?"—is a valid one. The answer, however, is
complicated. Explained here are ten different contributing factors.*

Cape Hatteras's geography is the main reason the surrounding waters
were given the famous nickname, the Graveyard of the Atlantic. It has
been an area to be avoided by mariners ever since the 1500s. The origin
of the phrase is unclear. It is often attributed to Alexander Hamilton
writing a letter to a friend, describing his harrowing voyage and the fact
that he saw so many skeletons of wrecked ships in this area. Historian
David Stick says, "Thus is formed the dreaded Diamond Shoals, its
fang-like shifting sand bars pushing seaward to snare the unwary mariner. Seafaring men call it the Graveyard of the Atlantic."[1]

In the 1970s, *National Geographic* magazine produced a map entitled "Ghost Fleet of the Outer Banks." The coastline was black with
silhouettes of wrecked ships, their names and dates of demise included.
As the site manager of the Chicamacomico Life-Saving Museum on

Outer Banks Shipwreck Map.
Sealake Products LLC

the Outer Banks, I have often witnessed visitors seeing this map for the first time. Invariably, there are two classic reactions: surprise or curiosity. The first usually elicits a loud exclamation of "Look at all those shipwrecks!" to no one in particular. I always interrupt and say, "And that is only one-third of the *known* shipwrecks!" When the visitor discovers that most experts at that time agreed on the (approximate) number of two thousand off Hatteras Island alone and as many as five thousand off the entire North Carolina coast, the second reaction is the most logical—asking the question "Why are there so many shipwrecks *here*?"

Why *So* Treacherous?

Several factors, some of which are unique to Cape Hatteras, are part of the complicated answer to that simple question.

Currents

It is a place where two major ocean currents converge. One current consists of the cold waters from the north, called the Labrador Current. They hug the North Atlantic shores from Baffin Bay in Canada, skirt around Newfoundland, and flow down US coastlines until reaching North Carolina. There these waters clash with the other mighty current, the Gulf Stream. That "river of warm water in the ocean," first discovered by Benjamin Franklin, is a marvel unto itself for many reasons. These two mighty currents don't just meet at Cape Hatteras; they explode there. The USCG Navigation Center, US Department of Homeland Security says on their website, "The circulation in the area where the Labrador Current and the Gulf Stream meet is one of the most complex and variable regions in the world."

Opposing Waves

If a person stands at "Cape Point" on a clear winter day, they will be treated to an unbelievable sight. Miles offshore, they will see giant white forms suddenly rising then slowly sinking into the ocean. These are gigantic waves, fifty to one hundred feet high and more, crashing into each other. We have always seen waves break 90 degrees to the shore, coming straight at us. But these waves meeting offshore are going parallel to the shore and in opposite directions, violently butting into each other. The energy in each collision is unfathomable. This goes on every few seconds for every minute of every hour of every day, year after year.

These wave explosions do more than just provide a spectacular show. Besides tons of water and energy, each wave is also carrying tons of loose sand. As the waves explode, sand "shrapnel" is randomly dispersed over a large area in all directions. This is gradually building and reshaping shoals (or underwater sand dunes and sandbars). Obviously, these shoals change with each wave explosion, making them impossible to accurately chart.

Diamond Shoals

Due to that massive and unrelenting amount of energy, the Diamond Shoals off Cape Hatteras extend as far as twenty miles (which is why the Cape Hatteras Lighthouse light reaches out this far). This means that twenty miles offshore, the water can be as shallow as four feet. At that distance, out of sight of the shore, one certainly does not expect such shallow depths. While affecting shipping to this day, this was a critical game-changer to the wooden sailing ships of old.

Conflicting Winds

The Cape Hatteras area, as we have seen, has two conflicting currents. It also has two conflicting prevailing winds. In summer, the prevailing and mostly constant winds are southwest (meaning, blowing from the southwest toward a northeast direction). In winter, they are northeast (the cause of winter storms, so-called nor'easters). Every time a captain left port along the Atlantic Coast, depending on if he was going south or north, and whether it was summer or winter, there would be a massive conflict of wind and current at some point. The large sailing ships of that day were unable to "tack" (zigzagging at angles to the oncoming wind) like sailboats today, so they became "dead in the water," sitting ducks for violent weather.

A Treacherous Choice

Could it get any more complicated? Yes. There was a seemingly simple choice each captain would have to make at the beginning of each voyage. The cold Labrador Current was close to shore and the warm Gulf Stream was considerably farther out. Consequently, the choice became to either stay close to shore, risking shoals and running aground, or to go out around the **Gulf Stream**. The second choice was certainly safer, but much longer, therefore taking more time. Safer, or quicker?

The Risk of Rushing

Hatteras Island juts far out into the **Atlantic**. Cape Hatteras is three hundred miles *east* of Jacksonville, Florida! Then, for ships' captains wanting to navigate around it, add another twenty miles. Too many captains tried to cut it too close by choosing the shorter route. Many ships have met with disaster while trying to save time.

No Safe Harbor

The Outer Banks are a nonstop string of barrier islands. That is precisely what they are: a barrier. There is no safe port along the entire 300-mile coast. Ships heading from New York Harbor to Jacksonville, Florida, for example, are tired and eager to reach their destination by the time they reach the North Carolina coast.

Unreliable Navigation

Many ships' captains of the time did not trust the simple and few navigation instruments available. As a result, their method was to always stay within sight of the shore. That worked well along many coasts, but not North Carolina's.

Storms

Cape Hatteras is famous for several things, but at the top of the list are storms. Although the mother of all Atlantic storms, the hurricane, is usually the first to come to mind, a simple thunderstorm could spell doom for an eighteenth-century wooden sailing ship. Hurricanes and nor'easters sent most ships to the Graveyard during this era. Remember, although there were some instruments on board, the chief weather forecasting method captains used on wooden sailing ships was scanning the horizon—three to five miles away. A deadly storm could be twenty miles away, only to be discovered too late.

The ship President *in gale, North Atlantic, 1841 (Lithograph, Currier & Ives).*
Public Domain

Shipwrecking Machines: German U-Boats

Germany did not invent the under-sea boat (later shortened to
"U-boat"), but they did perfect it. The idea had been around for some
time. Early submarines were unreliable, and most world navies never
took the idea seriously. But, by World War I, the U-boat was *the* ultimate stealth weapon: It could not be seen nor detected, so there was
no defense against it, and Germany relentlessly attacked America from
underwater between 1917 and 1918. Captured German documents
after the war told of German commanders laughing at how easy it was
to sink Allied ships, and how convenient for them, as the Americans
kept all their lights on at night, perfectly silhouetting the ships and
making them easy targets. It was so easy, in fact, that many U-boats
simply surfaced and fired their deck guns instead of using the expensive
torpedoes. It may have taken half an hour, but no one was shooting
back. Early American military intelligence had no explanation for why
all of these ships were suddenly sinking; the word *submarine* had never
come up.

Once again, the Wimble Shoals and the Diamond Shoals came into play. They created a very narrow, safe passage close to shore, making a perfect target zone. The Germans repeated this in World War II, calling it the "Great American Turkey Shoot." Although Germany lost nearly half of its almost 400 submarines, they nevertheless destroyed an astounding 2,600 Allied ships and took thousands of lives.

You would have thought that we would have learned something by World War II, but we had not. Once again, America was totally unprepared for the vicious German onslaught hidden beneath the waves. In 1942, during the first six months of the war, more than four hundred Allied ships were sunk, eighty-seven of those along the North Carolina coast. By this time, Cape Hatteras was being called "Torpedo Junction."

Carol White (now Dillon) of Buxton on Hatteras Island was just a girl when she inspired a popular World War II adventure novel. Carol's mother, the Buxton postmistress, reported to the FBI that a local German was mailing large, bulky, suspicious packages. Agents came and discovered that detailed North Carolina coastal maps were being sent to Germany. The local man was followed to New York, resulting in an entire gang of German spies being caught and executed. Young Carol's teacher, Nell Wise, dramatized the saga in the 1957 novel, *Taffy of Torpedo Junction*. The story follows thirteen-year-old Taffy Willis (based on Carol), who, with the help of her pony and dog, exposes a ring of Nazi spies operating from a secluded house on Hatteras Island.[2] Mrs. Dillon, now in her eighties, came to Chicamacomico every week during the summer for three years to mesmerize audiences with her memories of World War II on the Outer Banks. She remembers torpedoed explosions rocking the buildings and lighting up the night sky, and seeing actual German lifeboats onshore, empty, but with bullet holes.

II.

THE WELL KNOWN

CHAPTER 3
SS *MIRLO*

On August 16, 1918, surfman number eight of the Chicamacomico Life-Saving Station, Leroy Stockton Midgett, took the watch in the tower of the still-new 1911 station. Although this was three years after the Life-Saving Service had been re-created as the Coast Guard, these folks had been used to the old terminology for many years, and consequently continued to use it for some time.

On that beautiful August day there was extremely heavy surf lingering from a storm the day before. Leroy was nervous about his responsibility that day for two reasons, and the heavy surf was just one of them. The Coast Guard knew something civilians couldn't.

When World War I came to our shores in 1917, America was totally and completely unprepared. We had zero defenses for the ultimate stealth weapon of its day, the German submarine.

What Leroy did know was that the day before, German submarine *U-117* was seen on the surface of Chesapeake Bay, just miles north of Chicamacomico. She had been laying mines in the waters around one of America's largest navy bases. Worse yet, *U-117* was seen exiting the Chesapeake heading south—in the direction of Chicamacomico. The best guess at what would occur next was that *U-117* would probably head for the Wimble Shoals to lay more mines. These massive shoals just offshore created a very narrow shipping channel, making for a perfect target.

SS Mirlo *(actual photo).*
Courtesy US Coast Guard

At 4:00 p.m., looking out one of the south tower windows, Leroy spotted what he had been dreading all day: the British tanker SS *Mirlo*. He watched it slowly creep north, heading toward his station. By 4:30, the *Mirlo* was seven miles offshore, almost directly opposite the Chicamacomico Station. To his horror, Leroy saw a huge plume of water rise hundreds of feet into the air from the aft of the tanker, followed by an explosion so loud it shook the ground of his building and rattled its windows from seven miles away.

"Captain Johnny, a ship is in trouble!" he hollered out one of the open station tower windows. He was referring to John Allen Midgett Jr., the keeper (now called a chief bosun's mate), or officer in charge, of the station. One surfman was on leave on this day, and two were out sick, leaving the station short-staffed, with only five surfmen and Captain Johnny. These six hurried to the boathouse where Surfboat No. 1046 was kept. They rolled her out on a four-wheeled cart and attempted an immediate launch. But the surf was so heavy that it tossed the three-thousand-pound boat back up on the beach.

The *Mirlo* was carrying a full cargo load of 6,679 tons of gasoline, high-octane aviation fuel, and other petroleum products when the explosion happened. The commanding officer of the *Mirlo*, Captain William Williams, quickly ordered his ship west, trying to beach her, but he only got two miles when there was a second explosion. Captain

Williams knew he was in deep trouble, so he ordered his men to abandon ship.

Here is where the real quandary began: The *Mirlo* carried two lifeboats with a capacity of eighteen each, and she had a crew of fifty-one. The first lifeboat—filled to capacity—got away safely, and the crew began rowing for their lives at breakneck speed. The second lifeboat—also filled to capacity—attempted to launch, but as it was being lowered, it got fouled in the rigging, capsized, and dumped all of

THE CONTROVERSY

For years, there has been debate over the question: "Was it a torpedo or a mine?" Genuinely expert arguments have been put forth for each answer, so what is the layman to think? The most compelling evidence is the testimony of *Mirlo's* Captain Williams, saying that he reported a torpedo attack. Certainly, that should end the debate, but there is a language problem here, and Americans may have jumped to an understandable conclusion.

British English is not exactly the same as American. We know they say *lorry* for truck and *bonnet* for a car's hood, but some of the differences are not only confusing—they can be entirely misleading. For example, if a suspect testified under oath that he had hidden his weapon in his boot, Americans would go looking for his footwear. But if he was English, he'd have meant the trunk of his car.

Admiral David Glasgow Farragut (1801–1870) was the first senior officer of the US Navy at the time of the American Civil War. Aboard *Hartford*, Farragut entered Mobile Bay, Alabama, on August 5, 1864. Farragut gave the orders embodied by these famous words, "Damn the torpedoes. Full speed ahead." The torpedoes to which Farragut and his contemporaries referred would today be described as tethered mines.

Captain Williams was British. So, to him, *torpedo* may well have been what we call a mine. We know that is what *U-117* was laying there.

its occupants into the turbulent sea below. They were five miles offshore and probably didn't have a ghost of a chance of making landfall.

The biggest problem developed when a third explosion erupted. This earth-shaking blast ripped the *Mirlo* in two, releasing her entire explosive cargo of over six and a half thousand tons of gasoline, which, as we all know, floats—and will burn—on top of water. It ignited, and the resulting inferno was too large to properly describe, or even to imagine. One local newspaper's headline at the time simply read "Ocean Catches on Fire." By now it was 5:00 p.m. With all that noise, fire, and smoke, most of the men from the village of Rodanthe, and even lifesavers from the adjacent Gull Shoal Station to the south showed up. Even with their help, it took a full thirty minutes to finally launch through the raging surf.

After Surfboat No. 1046 got past the violent breakers, Captain Johnny could only see two things: a small lifeboat in the distance, full of survivors, and a wall of flames. Upon reaching the lifeboat, the captain learned that the rest of the crew were trapped in that inferno. Captain Johnny told the sailors to row close to shore but not attempt to land. He warned that as trained professionals, he and his crew had had a very difficult time getting though the treacherous surf. It would be a shame for the *Mirlo* sailors to have survived such a calamity only to drown getting ashore. He insisted they wait for the lifesavers.

Quickly then, Captain Johnny and his crew of five went out five miles and encountered a wall of flames, literally hundreds of feet tall. One contemporary author, Ray McAllister, wrote in his book *Hatteras Island: Keeper of the Outer Banks*, "What happened next was too implausible for any book or movie. What happened next could not have happened. Nonetheless, it did."[1]

As Captain Johnny's crew circled this huge wall of flames, suddenly, as if in a Hollywood movie, there was a break in the smoke and flames. Through this opening the surfmen could see an overturned lifeboat. Without hesitation, Captain Johnny turned Surfboat No. 1046 through the opening. The heat was so intense that it singed their facial hair, smoked their cork life vests, and blistered the paint on the boat.

As they approached, they found six men coming out from underneath the capsized lifeboat, scraping the flames aside, and gasping for a second or two of air. Their worst nightmare ended as they were pulled safely into Surfboat No. 1046 . . . or had it? Something was wrong. They should have been getting out of there with great haste; instead, they remained in the treacherous area. Captain Johnny knew full well that the British lifeboat would not have been launched with just six men, so he looked for the other sailors. The survivors told Captain Johnny that they had seen their shipmates go down—that they'd never come back up—and they urged him to get out of there. Even with that information, Captain Johnny and his crew continued to look for survivors in the inferno.

THE GRAND CROSS OF THE AMERICAN CROSS OF HONOR

In the early 1900s, Congress created the supreme medal for valor, the ultimate recognition for outstanding bravery. It was called the Grand Cross of the American Cross of Honor. It didn't matter whether the person was military or civilian, man or woman, black, white, or whatever. It was awarded for "extreme valor to the utmost degree." Consequently, the requirements were so lofty and stringent that rarely did anyone ever qualify for it; so, sadly, eventually it was dropped.

In its thirty-year reign, nationwide, only eleven were ever issued. Six of those recipients rowed together on August 16, 1918, in Chicamacomico's Surfboat No. 1046. That made it the *most highly awarded* maritime rescue in US history. That very boat is on display in Chicamacomico's 1874 Life-Saving Station. It is a testament to the Mighty Midgetts of Chicamacomico, whose sheer will, dedication, determination, and commitment rose above all others in the annals of lifesaving history. They would not be deterred, because that is just what they were born to do. That's why at Chicamacomico, I always said "The Midgetts are big around here!"

(Left to right) John Allen Midgett Jr., Arthur Midgett, Clarence Midgett, Leroy Midgett, Zion Midgett, and Prochorus Lee O'Neal each received the Grand Cross of the American Cross of Honor, the King George Medal, and the Gold Medal of the US Life-Saving Service. O'Neal was married to a Midgett!
Author's Photo

Finally realizing there were no more survivors left to find, the captain and his crew went back through the wall of flames and finally headed for shore. But the British sailors stopped him, explaining that when their ship had split in two, they had seen nineteen of their shipmates on the stern. It was engulfed in flames and was going down like a rock. If there was a sliver of a ray of hope, this was it: The stern is where the captain's launch is kept. It is not a lifeboat, just a small vessel for the captain and a few crewmen to go to shore—but at least it was something.

Indeed, it was. These were desperate men in a highly desperate situation, and it was all they had. They launched it. As soon as it hit the water, they discovered even more trouble. The small boat was far too overloaded, the water reaching to the gunnels and about to sink the small craft. Even worse, it was so crowded that there was no room to row, putting them at the mercy of the south wind, which carried deadly flames. Hearing this, Captain Johnny, already five miles offshore, took his crew of five, the six English sailors, and Surfboat No. 1046 a mile farther south, searching for more survivors. They went three miles, then six. Nine miles later, they came upon a small boat with nineteen men aboard—covered in oil, blistered and battered, but alive.

Captain Johnny took that boat in tow, struggled the nine miles back against the wind, met the other lifeboat they had instructed to wait, and began to ferry the survivors ashore, one boatload at a time. It took four trips. By nine p.m. that night, forty-two English sailors stood on the sands of Hatteras, alive due to the impossible heroics of the men of Chicamacomico.

After enduring a six-and-a-half-hour hellish ordeal and traveling a total of twenty-eight nautical miles in Surfboat No. 1046, the gallant crew of Chicamacomico had been successful. In his wreck report, Captain Johnny concluded, in a typical lifesaver understatement: "Returned to Station 11 p.m. Myself and crew very tired."

CHAPTER 4

RASMUS MIDGETT
AND THE *PRISCILLA*

Perhaps the most famous surfman and rescue on the Outer Banks. This single-handed rescue of ten men in the middle of the night, in the middle of a hurricane, after participating in three stations the day before, is the stuff of legend.

In the last year of the nineteenth century, the grueling rescue of a crew of ten from the barkentine *Priscilla* by surfman Rasmus Midgett remains one of the most dramatic, courageous, and daring rescues in the annals of the US Life-Saving Service, which would come to be called the US Coast Guard in 1915. Today this singular rescue remains upon a pedestal of Coast Guard history.

The place was Hatteras Island. Specifically, it was the Gull Shoal Life-Saving Station, located just south of the small village of Salvo. Rasmus Midgett was surfman number one at that station, next in line to become keeper. He also had served as surfman number one at the neighboring station to the north, Chicamacomico, home of the Mighty Midgetts of Chicamacomico. Rasmus would soon become the mightiest so far.

San Ciriaco Storm

The date was August 18, 1899. The most violent and destructive hurricane to ever hit the US Atlantic Coast until then was upon us. Newspapers and telegrams reported that the storm had wreaked havoc in the Caribbean, destroying thousands of homes and other buildings, killing hundreds of people, and sinking an armada of ships. It had passed over Puerto Rico on the feast of San Ciriaco, and would henceforth forever be known as the San Ciriaco Storm.

After leaving the Caribbean, it began leveling the Florida coast, and then moved slowly and relentlessly north. As it crawled up the Atlantic Coast, it took dead aim at Hatteras, striking the island on August 16 and raging for two days. In the end, seven vessels were lost as total wrecks on the beach; six more disappeared in the tumultuous seas without a trace. One of those that wrecked onshore was broken in two. The ten remaining persons on board huddled in their half of the 643-ton barkentine named *Priscilla*. Now it was the middle of the night, and they had no idea where they were. Surfman Rasmus Midgett, on beach patrol riding his horse, heard their cries of terror at 4:30 that morning. Then the impossible happened. Single-handedly, Rasmus Midgett saved all ten of those souls.

The Miraculous Rescue

As we have seen, US Life-Saving Service stations routinely had all beaches covered 24/7, but August 18 was not routine. Only a day and a half earlier, Rasmus Midgett was part of one of three teams responding to the inexplicable wreck of the *Aaron Reppard*—another story, told in chapter 10.

Naturally, these lifesaving crews were still exhausted the next day, but the storm raged on, and routine duties had to continue. A haggard and exhausted Rasmus drew one of the night beach patrols.

He left Gull Shoal Station at three a.m. on his personal horse. The tide was washing over the island, so he rode through the swash and rough surf. He passed one shipwreck hulk after the next from his previous experiences the day before. It was dark, loud, unpleasant, and difficult to see due to the lack of light and the blowing sand, rain, and sea spray. He had the wind in his face, so he must have smiled to himself, knowing that it would be at his back upon his return.

He soon spotted more flotsam and jetsam that *may* have been new since the day before. As he continued, he began to hear faint voices. His superior training and island instincts kicked in. Arriving at the wreck, he heard the terrified screams of survivors. They were huddled in the forward half of the barkentine *Priscilla*, which San Ciriaco had torn in two. Their half was nearly ashore. Still, it was the middle of the night and the middle of a violent hurricane, and those aboard were distressed and on the verge of panic. Already, Captain Springsteen's wife, two children, and the cabin boy had been swept away and disappeared forever.

Coast Guard painting of possible scene of Rasmus Midgett's impossibly heroic rescue of the crew of the barkentine Priscilla.
Courtesy US Coast Guard

Rasmus Midgett sitting on the Priscilla *after the rescue.*
Courtesy US Coast Guard

Rasmus was faced with a dilemma: It had taken him an hour and a half to reach this spot, and that was on his horse. According to "the Book" (the 200-page manual used by the USLSS), he was to return to the station and report the wreck. But that would take hours. The heavy rescue cart would likely not make it through the slush. On the other hand, were he to go in alone and get injured, or worse, they may all perish.

As a trained surfman, Rasmus observed that the waves were very high. The relationship between the height of a wave and the distance between them is called *wavelength*. The higher the waves are, the farther apart they are. Rasmus quickly devised a bold and daring plan.

He called out to the ship and instructed one person to jump off when he commanded. He would then run out between the waves, retrieve that person, and bring them safely to shore. It worked. He did that again and again. Seven times he risked his life to save another's. Imagine that distressing scene: dragging the soaking-wet weight of another human body through turbulent swash, fighting against wind, rain, and darkness, with no guarantee of survival.

Rasmus discovered three more on board who were too badly injured to take part in this plan. Nevertheless, he braved the gigantic waves an eighth time. After he struggled to climb aboard, he rested on the deck a few seconds to catch his breath and renew his strength. Then he picked up a survivor, climbed back down, timed the waves, and rushed the survivor to the beach. He did that all over again, an incredible two more times.

Rasmus Midgett saved all ten shipwreck survivors by himself—in the middle of a hurricane, in the middle of the night, after helping with rescues the day before.

CHAPTER 5

RICHARD ETHERIDGE
AND THE *E. S. NEWMAN*

*Fifteen years after the Civil War ended, overcoming racism was just part
of the job for the keeper of the all-black crew of the Pea Island Life-Saving
Station.*

Etheridge's Early Years

When there was suddenly an opening for keeper of the Pea Island Life-Saving Station, a surprising thing happened. The new keeper selected for the Pea Island Station was a local surfman from nearby Bodie Island Life-Saving Station by the name of Richard Etheridge. His appointment was surprising because up to that point he had only been surfman number six, the lowest-ranking surfman at the time. It was unheard of to be promoted from number six directly to the keeper position. Richard Etheridge was also black.

Etheridge was born a slave in 1842 into the household of John B. Etheridge on Bodie Island. Alongside John B.'s son, he lived in the master's house, worked with them, and was taught reading and writing by John B., a practice that was illegal at the time.

Etheridge enlisted in the Union Army shortly after the Civil War began. He served with the 32nd US Colored Troops, rising quickly to the rank of sergeant. Later Etheridge courageously challenged the

BODIE ISLAND

In most parts of the English-speaking world, b-o-d-i-e is pronounced "BOW-dee." There is a good reason, however, why here it is pronounced like the word "body." The tourist story is that it was because so many bodies washed ashore there from shipwrecks. Easy to believe.

But that's just one of many explanations. It's most likely the actual story (confirmed by a plaque in the lighthouse) is simply this: Originally it was an island owned by a man whose surname was Body. Even today, people confuse plural and possessive tenses. Someone in the 1700s scrawled a handwritten note on a map of the area calling it "Bodies Island," meaning, of course, "Body's Island." Remembering that literacy was very low then, everyone knew how to pronounce it, but few knew how it was spelled. Both mistakes have been retained to this day.

Union soldiers' rampant mistreatment of black refugees in the Freedmen's Colony on Roanoke Island.

Seeking a Career

Following the war, Etheridge briefly served as a Buffalo Soldier in the US Army in Texas. Returning to Bodie Island, he bought land on Roanoke Island, married, and became a father. Thus, a need arose for a secure job, something that wasn't plentiful at this time and place.

Etheridge had skills and knowledge from his boatman fishing days, and so proudly became surfman number six at the Bodie Island Life-Saving Station, part of what was known then as a "checkerboard" (or partially integrated) crew. Few black surfmen were ranked higher than number six.

When Etheridge was selected as the keeper in 1800, the white crew at Pea Island chose to quit rather than work under the authority of a black man. Even more tragically, soon after his appointment, the station mysteriously burned down.

Etheridge would not be deterred from his sworn duties. He oversaw the rebuilding of the station, and to form a crew, he had no choice but to hire black surfmen from other nearby checkerboard crews. Notably, Frank Newcomb, the white USLSS assistant superintendent who had originally recommended Etheridge, camped out where the new station was being built to prevent further trouble.

Etheridge's crew had to prove themselves to a very tough audience. This is best illustrated by their most famous rescue, of the schooner *E. S. Newman*. It was only one of the many responses by this station, and one of the six total wrecks there.

The Miraculous Rescue—Not by "the Book"

On the evening of October 11, 1896, the three-masted schooner *E. S. Newman* ran hard aground somewhere near the Pea Island Station. It was seven p.m., in the middle of a hurricane, with winds exceeding one hundred miles per hour. These torrents of wind enraged the Atlantic, producing gigantic waves and pushing ocean waters clear to the Pamlico Sound. It's said there was literally no visible land—the island was awash.

The ocean was far too violent to launch the surfboat, so the crew manned the only other rescue equipment they had—the beach cart. But when the cart reached the bottom of the ramp of the station, it mired down into several feet of overwash. With seemingly superhuman effort, the six surfmen, pushing and pulling their one-ton cart by manpower alone, sloshed through the tide and spindrift until they reached the wreck site. Upon arrival, the surfmen heard from the ship what was later officially described in the records as "the voice of gladdened hearts."

Exhausted and desperate, the surfmen attempted to mound up sands below the water as a perch for the Lyle gun. The 200-pound cannon simply sank. They were now out of standard rescue methods, so Keeper Etheridge proposed a bold, daring, and nearly impossible plan. He asked for two volunteers, and two surfmen immediately stepped forward. One was Theodore Meekins, who had originally spotted the wreck. The plan was to tie a stout rope around the two men, with the end of the rope to be anchored by the remaining surfmen onshore. These two would carry another line with them and swim out into the deadly breakers. Why two surfmen tied together? In case one (or both) drowned. No man left behind; they would have a proper burial.

Indeed, they did go out, and miraculously, they reached the broken ship. On board was Captain Sylvester A. Gardiner, his wife, their three-year-old son, Tommy, and a crew of six. The surfmen had formed a human breeches buoy from ship to shore. The first line was tied around the terrified little Tommy, and he was taken ashore successfully. Next his mother and then the rest of the crew were rescued. Following nautical tradition, Captain Gardiner was last.

One by one, all were safely landed off the wreck by nine p.m., but they were still a long way from safety. The seemingly impossible rescue finally concluded at one a.m. when all reached the Pea Island Station. As at all stations, the survivors were given sustaining food, water, and complimentary dry clothes, always on hand at every station.

Normally, rescues involving such extraordinary bravery and heroics were rewarded with Life-Saving Service medals: silver for extraordinary bravery, and gold for extreme bravery. This was surely extreme bravery, but the Pea Island crew received no medals—at least, not yet.

The Pea Island Station in Context

The station neighboring Pea Island to the north was Oregon Inlet, and to the south was Chicamacomico, and, for a while, New Inlet. These stations were manned by white men, and they interacted with Etheridge's black crew many times each day during beach patrol. It was common practice to assist your neighboring station during actual rescues.

From 1878 to 1906, Pea Island assisted (or was assisted by) Oregon Inlet, Chicamacomico, and New Inlet—eleven times for total wrecks, and hundreds more for partial wrecks, groundings, or warnings.

RESCUES OF TOTAL-LOSS
SHIPWRECKS BY
PEA ISLAND STATION
AND NEIGHBORING STATIONS

M & E Henderson	1879	Chicamacomico and New Inlet (same storm, same place)
Mary L. Vankirk	1882	Chicamacomico and New Inlet (same storm, and three more ships)
Lizzie S. Haynes	1889	New Inlet
Annie E. Blackman	1889	New Inlet
Irene Thayer	1892	Oregon Inlet
Emma C. Cotton	1895	Oregon Inlet
James Woodall	1896	Chicamacomico and New Inlet
Maggie Lawrence	1896	Oregon Inlet
Jane C. Harris	1900	Oregon Inlet
Montana	1904	New Inlet
Jennie Lockwood	1906	Oregon Inlet

This does not include the possibly hundreds of assists to ships by this station during its existence from 1878 to 1947, whose ships were then able to carry on. Additionally, Pea Island Station assisted neighboring stations with numerous successful assists.

It was through these contacts that each race learned about the other, that they were only men, with much in common. Both came to recognize and accept the realities, not the images. They knew each other by their same work, and soon knew each other by name, each other's families, and characteristics.

Only fifteen years after the Civil War, positive race relations had begun deep in the South on the remote Outer Banks of North

The classic—and only known—photograph of the Pea Island crew in front of their 1878 Life-Saving Station before it burned down. "Captain" Richard Etheridge, station keeper, is at far left.
Courtesy US Coast Guard

Carolina. While that was well over one hundred years ago, they are lessons still valid today.

Belated Bestowal of Gold Medals

In 1995, Katie Burkhart, a fourteen-year-old white student in a North Carolina school, had chosen for her social studies project a report on the all-black Pea Island Life-Saving Station. She was amazed that it was so little known at that time, because she found it fascinating. When she reached the part about the incredible *E. S. Newman* rescue of October 11, 1896, she was appalled to discover that the Pea Island crew had never received any awards simply because they were African-American. She wrote to her North Carolina senator, Jessie Helms, and also to

President Bill Clinton. She realized that the one hundredth anniversary was fast approaching. With the help of many, spearheaded by Rear Admiral Stephen Rochon, on March 5, 1996, descendants of that 1896 crew were awarded Coast Guard Life-Saving Gold Medals in a fitting formal ceremony.

The Etheridge Legacy

Richard Etheridge's farm and land were on Roanoke Island far from town at that time, in a location upon which the North Carolina Aquarium on Roanoke Island was later built. Workers discovered the family graveyard of Richard Etheridge while tearing down a World War II US Navy infirmary to make way for the aquarium. The cemetery has stood near the aquarium's entrance for more than forty years. Efforts to integrate the cemetery more fully into the aquarium coincided with a yearlong renovation in 2016.

James Melvin, a Nags Head artist, became interested in Richard Etheridge and the Pea Island Life-Saving Station in the early 1980s. In 1985, Melvin worked with Rhett White, then director of the North Carolina Aquarium on Roanoke Island, on a grant proposal to the Z. Smith Reynolds Foundation to fund the creation of a permanent exhibit of his paintings, immortalizing the surfmen of Pea Island.

Hurricane Irene in 2011 was one of Hatteras Island's most devastating. The enormous power of the wind, water, and waves actually sliced completely through the island in two spots just north of the village of Rodanthe. The North Carolina Department of Transportation (NCDOT) filled in the new gap immediately north of the village, but decided to build a bridge over the next one, five and a half miles farther north.

This was almost exactly where the 1878 (and rebuilt 1880) Pea Island Life-Saving Station had been located. NCDOT had installed a temporary bridge locally referred to as the Lego Bridge while construction of a permanent bridge took place. The final new bridge was named for and dedicated to Captain Richard Etheridge in 2018.

This attractive bridge holds one more unique distinction: It is the only place on the entire island where travelers on NC Highway 12 can view the Atlantic Ocean and the Pamlico Sound at the same time!

We salute you, Captain Richard Etheridge.

CHAPTER 6
G. A. KOHLER

One of the last great wooden sailing ships to wreck on the Outer Banks. Part of the skeleton of the huge four-masted schooner is one of the few remaining visible shipwrecks on the Hatteras Island beaches today.

Outer Banks Showpiece

The most persistent Outer Banks shipwreck which performs a disappearing and reappearing act is the *G. A. Kohler*. Every resident of Hatteras Island, and many of its regular visitors, can tell you exactly where it is and when it last appeared (just over Ramp 27, immediately to the left).

SCHOONER

Often, landlubbers call all sailing vessels with tall masts *ships*. Technically, that's like calling all cars *Fords*. A ship is one specific type of vessel (there are a total of twelve), each one a different variation of masts, sails, and rigging. A schooner like the *G. A. Kohler* is defined by Merriam-Webster as "a typically two-masted fore-and-aft rigged vessel with a foremast and a taller mainmast stepped nearly amidships." There was only one class of schooner larger than the *G. A. Kohler*.

The *G. A. Kohler* has another distinction: It was one of the last great shipwrecks on the Outer Banks. David Stick, Outer Banks's most renowned historian, expressed it best: "For almost ten years after she came ashore in the hurricane of 1933, the four-masted schooner *G. A. Kohler*, bulking majestically in her last resting place high above the shore, was one of the showpieces of the Outer Banks."[1]

The Ship

The 1,488-gross-ton ship was built in 1919 at the American (Railroad) Car & Foundry at the Christina River Shipyards in Wilmington, Delaware. It was one of the last huge workhorse ships delivering cargo from the Atlantic Coast.

KALMAR NYCKEL

The *Kohler* has a famous neighbor. It is the *Kalmar Nyckel*, also built in Wilmington, Delaware. She is Delaware's Tall Ship Ambassador. The *Nyckel* looks like a ship from the seventeenth century, but in fact is much younger than the *Kohler*, having been built in 1997. A full-rigged ship based on the first Swedish ship to arrive in America in 1638, she landed in what is now the state of Delaware. The *Kalmar Nyckel* is a gorgeous replica. If you have the chance to see her, don't miss it!

Kohler's Final Voyage

The *G. A. Kohler* sailed from the pier of the Redman-Vane Company of Baltimore, Maryland, bound for Haiti. The sailing of August 20, 1933, began on a beautiful summer day. Unfortunately, the sun was not shining in Bermuda the next day, where a Category 4 hurricane raged. On August 23, the storm made landfall on the Outer Banks of North Carolina. This sixth storm of the year 1933 would become a benchmark for the Atlantic Coast.

How much knowledge Captain George Hopkins had of this storm before his departure from Baltimore is not documented. It has been a maritime tradition for sailing ships to consider storms as part of the job. Captain Hopkins may well have felt confident that his monster of a ship could easily handle any storm; however, this hurricane turned out to be a far greater monster than he could have imagined.

Official records report that the *G. A. Kohler* was seen wallowing help-lessly just south of Coast Guard Station Gull Shoal located south of the present-day village of Salvo on Hatteras Island. Gull Shoal notified her sister station of Chicamacomico in the adjacent Rodanthe village, and both crews responded. The *Kohler* ran hard aground extremely high on the beach early in the morning of Wednesday, August 23. That was when the full fury of the storm hit the Outer Banks, with winds of up to ninety miles per hour.

With seas and winds both so high, conditions made it impossible for Coast Guard crews to physically respond. The dunes we know today weren't built until 1937, which explains why the *Kohler* ended up so high on the beach. The shipwreck's remains don't seem to be as far up the beach today because of erosion and migration. The island is slowly moving west.

Coast Guard crews helplessly watched the insurmountable, typically violent weather throughout the entire day and into the night. *Kohler* sailors were sending distress signal flares and signal flags from their stricken ship, but the blinding weather made it impossible for the Coast

HATTERAS ISLAND AND OCRACOKE SAND DUNES

Most visitors to Hatteras Island are not aware that the protective dunes they cross to get to the beach are not natural. The dunes were a make-work Depression-era project of the Civilian Conservation Corps (CCC) that started in 1937 and was initially completed in 1941. The process continues today.

The much-reproduced classic photograph of the beached schooner, G. A. Kohler.
Courtesy National Park Service, Cape Hatteras National Seashore

Guard to see. Chief bosun's mate and officer in charge of the Chicamacomico Station, John Allen Midgett Jr., led both crews the next morning. Aboard the *Kohler* were Captain Hopkins, his wife, a crew of eight sailors, and a dog. All were safely brought to shore using the Lyle gun and breeches buoy.

When the hurricane finally passed and the wind and seas had gradually subsided, the schooner was found to be ridiculously inland on the beach. It was so far dug in, in fact, that there was no possibility of refloating her gargantuan frame. There remained only one option—to leave it there. It could hardly have been a tourist attraction at that time. There was no NC Highway 12. There was no bridge to the island. There were few hotels or rental houses. While this meant there were very few tourists at the time, the wreck was popular with the locals. Amazingly, Captain Hopkins sold the ship to island resident Charles T. Williams II of Avon for $150.00. Interviewed by a local student magazine, Williams said that it was the most beautiful ship he had ever laid eyes on.

The *G. A. Kohler* remained a complete ghost ship for the next ten years. In 1943, the US government burned the entire hulk to salvage the iron fittings as part of the efforts for World War II. Ironically, what little remains is now a tourist attraction. Powerful storms over the years alternately bury her with sand or wash the sand away, exposing the wreck. When it is visible, it is one of the few shipwrecks remaining on any Outer Banks beach.

A visit from a descendant of the Kohler family, who owned the schooner, even made the local newspaper:

Kohler Family Visit to Chicamacomico

The Hagen family from Kent, Washington, recently visited the Chicamacomico Life-Saving Station Historic Site, and Mrs. Linda Hagen [...] identified herself as the great-granddaughter of George Alfred Kohler.

Kohler had a profitable cigar factory in the town of Yoe, PA, that allowed him to have a four-masted, 1,462-ton schooner built in 1919 which he owned and christened the *G. A. Kohler*.[2]

Local stories abound and are still proudly told to anyone willing to listen. Mary Gray of Avon gave an oral history interview on July 28, 1988, and mentioned that her mother got some furniture and mahogany chairs from the ship. Dallas Miller had a desk from the *Kohler* which he graciously donated to the Graveyard of the Atlantic Museum. Salvaging materials from shipwrecks was not unusual; in fact, it was an especially common practice in the earliest years of the island for residents to build the foundations of their homes from salvaged ship timbers.

Joe Schwarzer, director of the North Carolina Maritime Museums, put it most clearly when he said that shipwrecks on Hatteras Island in those days "were like Walmart coming ashore!" Due to the length of many voyages, ships were fitted with many household goods: tables, chairs, cutlery, lanterns, candlesticks, tools, barrels, and more. Shipwrecks delivered these items right to the islanders' doors.

The hurricane of 1933 made a great and lasting impression on the *G. A. Kohler*, which, in turn, made a great and lasting impact on Hatteras Island.

CHAPTER 7
HMS *BOUNTY*

On the morning of Monday, October 29, 2012, television newscasters announced that the HMS Bounty *was sinking. What? Locals wondered if they could possibly mean the famous movie ship from the 1962 MGM film* Mutiny on the *Bounty, starring Marlon Brando and Trevor Howard. That HMS* Bounty? *No way. As further details followed, it turned out to be exactly that ship.*

The Ship's Story

This *Bounty* (technically, not the HMS, because it was not a Royal Navy ship) was inspired by the 1790 ship of the same name which was famously burned and sunk after a true-life mutiny. The new *Bounty* was built in 1960 by MGM for their 1962 film, *Mutiny on the* Bounty, and would become the most expensive movie set ever made, at the time. It was a 412-ton, three-masted, full-rigged ship, at 169 feet long and 30 feet wide, with a draft of 13 feet. She was built in Nova Scotia by the Smith & Rhuland Shipyard, specifically for the movie. The ship followed the design of the original very closely, but was wider in certain places to accommodate camera crews. Since it would not be carrying paying passengers, MGM asked the Coast Guard to designate the *Bounty* as an "Uninspected Vessel," which would allow it to set sail without passing standard safety checks.

The original movie script called for the ship to be burned at the end, but Marlon Brando refused to finish the film if they destroyed the actual ship. So it survived. After filming, the *Bounty* spent the next twenty-one years in St. Petersburg, Florida, as a popular tourist attraction. In 1986, media mogul and millionaire Ted Turner purchased the entire MGM vintage library for his Turner Classic Movies TV network. When he learned that the purchase included the actual ship, he was not prepared to maintain it, so donated it to the Tall Ship Bounty Foundation. There, its popularity grew even more. Its work in Hollywood spanned many years, appearing in the films *Yellowbeard* (1983), *Treasure Island* (1990), *Pirates of the Caribbean: Dead Man's Chest* (2006), and the 2007 *Pirates of the Caribbean: At World's End*. Once it became part of its own foundation, with Captain Robin Walbridge at the helm, it made numerous transatlantic trips and sailed educational voyages to ports all over the world.

An Ill-Fated Voyage

In the fall of 2012, as Hurricane Sandy threatened the shores of North Carolina, the *Bounty*'s Captain Robin Walbridge decided to put to sea, saying the ship was safer there than in port. The entire volunteer crew agreed. Walbridge gave anyone who wanted to leave the right to do so, saying he wouldn't think any less of them if they did. No one opted out. The *Bounty* was scheduled to appear in St. Petersburg, Florida, soon anyway, so why not get there early, and safe? Volunteer crewman Josh Scornavacchi said they had "complete faith" in the captain and the ship, and that both "had been in much worse storms."

But the wooden ship was fifty-two years old and, as later discovered, in very poor condition. Problems with bilge (water) pumps had been reported, but were not addressed. On calm voyages, it normally took on two feet of water in the bilge. "All wooden ships are always sinking," said crew member Douglas Fount. Since the *Bounty* operated as a recreational vessel, no safety inspections were required for the ship to go to sea because the *Bounty* carried no passengers.

According to Scornavacchi, the weather was "pretty nice" when they left port in Connecticut on the morning of Thursday, October 25, 2012. But "it got bad pretty quickly." Soon, they were experiencing eighty-knot winds and seas from six to twelve feet. At 9:00 p.m., the *Bounty* sent a distress signal to the Coast Guard base in Wilmington, North Carolina, saying they were 120 miles off the North Carolina coast, and that they were taking on water and listing to starboard.

The Coast Guard jumped into action. The first thing they had to do was locate the stranded crew amid hurricane conditions. An HC-130J Hercules airplane was launched from Air Station Elizabeth City. On the way to the rescue, Coast Guard HC-130J Hercules pilot Mike Myers received a radio transmission from the *Bounty*: "They had lost two generators and therefore could no longer bail water; [they had] lost e-mail communications; and now [they] had six feet of water in the ship's hold, and it was increasing at a rate of two more feet every hour." At 4:26 a.m. on October 26, reports came in that Walbridge had ordered the crew to abandon ship.

The Hercules was the first sign of salvation for *Bounty*'s survivors. The aircraft kept watch over the adrift sailors through the night, deploying flares, additional life rafts, and a self-locating datum marker buoy, a device that helps the Coast Guard measure surface currents to aid in the search for survivors.

As the Hercules circled as sentry, at 5:30 a.m., Coast Guard Base Air Station Elizabeth City launched rescue helicopter CG6012, piloted by Lt. Cmdr. Steve Cerveny, to begin rescue operations. Lt. Stephanie Young gave this account: "Wearing night-vision goggles, the helicopter raced to the scene amidst heavy rain and powerful winds. They had to fly low, at about 300 feet, to stay below the clouds, and arrived on scene just after sunrise Monday morning. It didn't take long before they spotted a survivor in the water, adrift and alone."[1]

This was eerie, because there was nothing else visible around this one person. Copilot Lt. Jane Peña spotted the strobe lights attached to the survivor's suit. Due to the extreme winds and heavy seas, it took several attempts and techniques to get the rescue basket positioned exactly how they wanted it. Soon Petty Officer 2nd Class Randy Haba, the crew's rescue swimmer, was pulling *Bounty* survivors out of the life raft and bringing them safely aboard the H-60 Jayhawk helicopter.

"Peña recalls looking out at this point and seeing another strobe in the distance. It was the sunken ship, with only its three masts sticking out. With the crew of the CG6012 focused on getting the survivors out of one life raft, rescue helicopter CG6031 arrived on scene ready to rescue survivors from the second life raft, piloted by Lt. Cmdr. Steve Bonn,"[2] Young said.

But the helicopters had their own problems. Peña's H-60, No. GC6012, had only one hour left before they would have to return to the Elizabeth City base to refuel. And both helos were also fighting to maintain proper altitude as the storm waves were cresting at thirty feet!

Bonn quickly found the second life raft, although it was a mile away from the first. Then, the best-known moment of the rescue occurred:

> Rescue swimmer Petty Officer 3rd Class Dan Todd was deployed. Todd swam to the raft and in a particularly calm, candid moment greeted the survivors with, "Hi, I'm Dan. I heard you guys need a ride." When we show up, it's the worst day of these survivors' lives; using an icebreaker like that helps them relax, knowing that we're in control, and that this is just another day for us, said Todd. It was good that we got to go help people. We were just doing the job.[3]

Coast Guard rescuers worked past the point of exhaustion to evacuate fourteen of the sixteen crewmen from life rafts to nearby helicopters amid the turbulent wind and waves. Missing were crew Claudene Christian and Captain Robin Walbridge. Ironically, Claudene claimed she was related to Fletcher Christian of the original mutiny on the *Bounty*.

Scornavacchi summarized it stoically: "Without the Coast Guard, none of us would be here . . . This ship had touched so many people, and it's gone."[4]

Site operations manager Linda Molloy introduces Coast Guard presenters from Air Station Elizabeth City for one of four presentations of their Bounty *rescue at Chicamacomico LSS Station, 2013.*
Author's photo

Subsequent aircrafts were sent out and Coast Guard cutters USCGC *Elm* and USCGC *Gallatin* were diverted to the scene in search of the two missing sailors. Christian would be recovered seven nautical miles from the vessel's original reported position and found to be deceased. Several days later—after searching more than ninety hours and covering twelve thousand overlapping square nautical miles in the Atlantic

"MAYDAY"

I have often wondered why "Mayday" is called to signal distress. Why not "Mother's Day" or "New Year's Day"? Turns out, it's not that kind of May Day. It came from a time when French had been designated the official international language. If you understand that language, it suddenly makes sense. *Aider* is the French word for "to help," and "help me" in French would be *M'aider*, pronounced "Mayday."

Ocean since the *Bounty*'s crew abandoned ship—the search for *Bounty*'s captain, Robin Walbridge, was called off.

You can listen to personal accounts from the survivors and rescuers in the Weather Channel documentary[5] about the event.

Seeking Answers: The Coast Guard Investigation

The US Coast Guard's report, released by the National Transportation Safety Board (NTSB) in February 2014, determined that the *Bounty* tragedy was largely caused by Walbridge's "reckless decision to sail . . . into the well-forecast path of Hurricane Sandy." If the management and the captain of the sunken tall ship *Bounty* had "exercised the proper responsibility, judgment and prudence," the deaths of two people would have been prevented.[6]

The Coast Guard severely chastised Captain Walbridge for undertaking its final voyage in the face of an impending hurricane. They said this was the "most critical" cause of the sinking.[7]

Worse than merely going out to sea in a hurricane, Walbridge carelessly decided to play with it, risking all. As evidence, the Coast Guard introduced a YouTube video of Walbridge where he said, "We chase hurricanes." In the video, Walbridge explained how to "get a good ride" out of a hurricane by sailing "as close to the eye of it as you can," staying behind the storm in its southeast quadrant.

The report said that this grave error was fatally compounded by the "decision to order the crew to abandon the ship much too late."

Many of Walbridge's questionable decisions seem to be the result of misplaced passion and hubris. He had mastered this singular ship for seventeen years and was almost single-handedly responsible for its continued existence. His passion did not allow him to believe the ship would not survive after all it had been through.

Richard Bailey, captain of a similar tall ship, the HMS *Rose*, was an admirer of Walbridge's skill, competence, and experience. "I was more surprised that he, of all the people who might be lost, that it was he and the *Bounty*."

A further perfect storm of ingredients sealed the fate of the *Bounty* and crew.

The ship's owner, the HMS *Bounty* Organization LLC, according to the report, "committed acts of negligence." Shipyard workers at the *Bounty*'s homeport had only months before warned Walbridge about serious rot in hull planks, both port and starboard, and even more critically, in her frames, or "ribs."

Fatigue and inexperience also contributed to the disaster, the report said. The "crew was suffering from fatigue, which was born out of lack of sleep, being seasick, and from the physical exertion of fighting to save the vessel while in extreme weather conditions for over twenty-four hours." The report noted that of the fifteen crew members, ten had less than one year's experience aboard the *Bounty*.

Without a doubt, the captain's harshest critic at the hearing was Jan Miles, one of the world's most respected tall-ship pilots, and a self-described friend of Walbridge. Captain of the *Pride of Baltimore II*, Miles summed up Walbridge's actions in four words: "reckless in the extreme."

CHAPTER 8

QUEEN ANNE'S REVENGE

There was no more famous a pirate than Ocracoke Island's Blackbeard, with his notorious flagship, the Queen Anne's Revenge. *The 1996 discovery of that 1718 shipwreck was one of the ultimate, real buried treasure finds.*

All of the other stories in this book are about people rescuing people from shipwrecks. This one is the exception, as it's about people rescuing a shipwreck—in fact, one of the most famous shipwrecks in the world, which caused a furor in the news when it was discovered. It was the flagship of the notorious pirate Blackbeard—the *Queen Anne's Revenge*.

It is easy to understand why piracy appealed to English lads in the 1700s. Many were orphans or products of brothels, like the street urchins portrayed in Charles Dickens's *Oliver Twist*. These young boys literally had to beg or steal on city streets every day just to stay alive. The ones in port cities were in constant contact with sailors, many of whom were actual pirates who also made their living stealing—just from far wealthier victims.

The Backstory: A Brief Summary

Eighteenth-Century Piracy

Almost everybody has heard of Blackbeard the pirate. A major frustration for historians and scholars researching histories before and after the 1700s is that facts ebb and flow like the tides, constantly changing or even swirling around like grains of sand on windswept beaches.

Additional factors help blur fact and fiction in historical research of this period. There was the extremely low literacy rate of most European populations at the time, further complicated by the lack of a standard language or even standard spelling. The classic example, even earlier, is that Sir Walter Raleigh spelled his own name twenty-seven different ways, none of which we use today! Eighteenth-century fake news further blurs the record. Often written or published accounts of the day were intended to purposely trick an adversary, or were politically motivated, or were invented to give an enemy false information.

Blackbeard the Pirate

As a result, a great deal of the information about Blackbeard the pirate is unclear, confusing, and even contradictory. His name has been written in the records of his day as Edward Teach, Thatch, Thache, and Edouard Titohe—all aliases. Most probably, he was Edward Drummond from Bristol, England, most commonly known as Teach.

He first appeared in official records when he joined Captain Benjamin Hornigold's crew in 1716, a well-known English pirate. In all likelihood, he was a sailor and privateer for the English during the War of Spanish Succession, also known as Queen Anne's War (1701–1713). That amount of experience would have trained him well in ship handling, war, and combat.

In 1717, Hornigold retired from piracy and promoted Teach as captain of his own ship. Records indicate that Teach was also associated with another pirate during this time, Stede Bonnet.

Soon Blackbeard was actively and successfully engaged in pirate activities throughout the Caribbean. His subsequent exploits are well documented. In the fall of 1717, off the island of Martinique, just before he retired, Hornigold joined Blackbeard and his crew to capture what would be Teach's greatest prize of all—*La Concorde*. This French slave ship was a 300-ton vessel with a crew of seventy-five and armed with sixteen cannons. This ship is the main focus of our upcoming story.

PRIVATEER VS. PIRATE

Far too often, one hears the definition of a "privateer" as "legalized piracy." There is a substantial difference. We all know that a pirate was usually a low-class scoundrel who resorted to criminal activity by stealing ships and their valuables. In spite of England's reputation during that era—"Britannia rules the waves"—this was not the case in the early 1700s. The English navy was grossly outnumbered by Spanish troops, their archrival at the time. To bolster her armed maritime fleet, England proposed a simple idea: to arm private merchant ships. The incentive was that by attacking *enemy ships of our nation only*, the merchant ship would receive a share of the bounty. To be official, these merchants were issued formal documents of government permission, called Letters of Marque. The privateers were strictly forbidden to attack any other ships; moreover, they would suffer serious consequences for withholding booty. It is likely both of these transgressions nevertheless happened frequently.

Therefore, to equate a privateer to a pirate would be analogous to saying an American soldier eliminating terrorists is a common criminal.

Blackbeard renamed *La Concorde* the *Queen Anne's Revenge*, probably because of his negative experiences in Queen Anne's War. *La Concorde* was built in England in 1710 (during Queen Anne's War) and originally named *Concord*. The next year she was captured by the French and renamed *La Concorde de Nantes*. This large ship was modified to hold even more cargo, especially slaves, as the slave trade between Europe, Africa, and the West Indies was extremely profitable.

Blackbeard's Flagship on the Loose

In re-outfitting the *Queen Anne's Revenge* (nowadays often designated simply *QAR*), Blackbeard added forty more cannons, making it one of the most formidable ships of all time.

WHAT IS A PIRATE SHIP?

There is no such thing as a pirate ship. Calling a vessel a pirate ship would be like calling the generic getaway vehicle in a robbery a thief's car. Pirates simply used ships of that day for their exploits. While it's true that they often modified these ships for their own purposes—more armaments, increased cargo holds, cut-down sides, etc.—these were still simply ships of that time period. We often hear people refer to any sailing ship—sloop, brigantine, frigate, schooner, bark—of the 1600s, 1700s, or 1800s as a pirate ship. They are all simply sailing ships.

His growing power allowed him to plunder almost all of the Caribbean Islands. His second prize was the capture of the sloop *Adventure*. In possession of his flagship and a fleet of three smaller sloops, he brazenly blockaded the port of Charlestown, South Carolina, and held it hostage for one week before his demands were met (he was merely asking for just a chest of medicine).

Shortly after that, the *QAR* and *Adventure* ran aground and sank in what is now called Beaufort Inlet, near Morehead City, North Carolina. This is where our story about the discovery and recovery of the ship *QAR* begins.

First, however, some closing thoughts on Blackbeard the Pirate.

Amazingly, there are no records or reports of Blackbeard ever killing anyone during his entire career, until his final battle. How and why, then, did he ever get the fierce reputation so often expressed, as in the following quote from *The Telegraph* of December 6, 2008? "He was history's most feared pirate, striking terror into seafarers as he cut a blood-thirsty swathe through the Caribbean and North Atlantic."[1]

Quite simply, he created that reputation himself. He was a large, strapping man, well over six feet tall. He had grown a long, thick, unruly beard, dark black in color. His "battle dress" consisted of all-black clothes with a large black captain's hat. Across his chest, he strapped two crossed belts of loaded pistols. He inserted slow-burning cannon fuses under his hat and lit them. There are numerous reports and quotes of his appearance "being that of the Devil himself." Can you imagine being confronted with this image of a madman? His victims automatically surrendered without resistance.

Just like today, there were variations in punishment for theft versus murder. The only thing pirates wanted was wealth; logically, it was senseless to commit murder and be hanged for it if caught, since theft carried only a jail sentence. So, Edward Teach created the imaginary persona of Blackbeard, the *terrible* pirate. He was, in fact, one of the first international terrorists. His weapon was creating terror, which in and of itself helped to spread his fierce reputation.

Blackbeard's End

Most people have the impression that Blackbeard's career must have lasted many years in order to gain such notoriety. It lasted, in fact, only eighteen months. Since the governor of North Carolina, Charles Eden, supported the pirate for a share of his booty, it was the neighboring governor of Virginia, Alexander Spotswood, who sent an armed contingent to confront and stop this pirate. Royal Navy Lieutenant Robert Maynard led the attack and ignited an epic battle of hand-to-hand combat on the deck of the *Queen Anne's Revenge* worthy of a Hollywood movie. Blackbeard was finally killed by five bullet wounds and twenty sword cuts. Blackbeard was famously decapitated, and his head hung from the bowsprit of Maynard's sloop as it sailed back to Virginia. This was intended to serve as a strong message to all remaining pirates along the East Coast. It worked. The Golden Age of Piracy on the Atlantic Coast ended soon afterward, by the 1720s.

Queen Anne's Revenge

There is controversy over whether Blackbeard intentionally or accidentally ran his flagship aground and left her to sink. The prevailing argument was that it was intentional, supported by the fact that his company had grown to three hundred pirates with a flotilla of ships. Perhaps too much to oversee and control? Especially considering the typical personality of a lawless pirate crewman. What is known is that following the abandonment of the *QAR*, Blackbeard set most of the crew on a small island in the inlet and departed Beaufort with a handpicked crew and most of the valuable plunder. Were those sailors heartlessly marooned, or thoughtfully saved from drowning? They were a mile from shore, and most people in those days, even sailors, did not know how to swim. Marooned or saved? Depends on how one looks at it.

The other argument—that the *QAR*'s sinking was accidental—is supported by evidence such as Jasper Copping's article in the *Telegraph*, on December 6, 2008.[2] Marine archaeologists diving on the wreck discovered a large pile of heavy ballast in the middle section of the ship. This included anchors and cannon that obviously had no business being there. It would make sense, however, if an able seafarer like Blackbeard was trying to refloat his vessel. Moving that much weight from the front of the ship—the part that first ran aground—to farther back would raise the bow and perhaps release the stricken ship.

Further evidence was the discovery of an anchor 450 feet away in front of the ship, which could be an indication that a technique called "kedging" might have been used. This was a common method of moving a sailing ship if it were not sailing, and was used especially to go upstream to harbor in narrow rivers. Here is how kedging worked: The anchor and line would be rowed out ahead of the ship in a small ship's boat called a "longboat," and then dropped. Using the capstan (a large winch whose sole purpose on a sailing ship was to move heavy objects, such as yards and anchors), the ship was then winched up to the kedge anchor. The anchor was then hauled up to the longboat, which was rowed farther out and dropped again. The process was repeated until the ship reached its desired destination.

Kedging might have been employed with the *QAR* in an effort to refloat and save the ship. After all, Blackbeard had only had the mighty

QAR for eight months. He had created "the most formidable pirate ship" of all time, the mere sight of which struck terror into its potential victims. In those short eight months, Blackbeard had captured forty-five ships—all without any killing. So, why would he scuttle such an amazing, powerful, and unique weapon?

Discovery of the *Queen Anne's Revenge*

On March 3, 1997, in a joint news conference with the shipwreck salvage company Intersal Inc. from Florida and the North Carolina Department of Natural and Cultural Resources (NCDNCR), North Carolina governor Jim Hunt announced the discovery of what appeared to be Blackbeard's flagship, the *Queen Anne's Revenge*. It was in the right place; it was the right size; it seemed to be from the correct time period; and it was heavily armed and filled with artifacts.[3]

Amazingly, the wreck was found in only about twenty feet of water. Mike Daniel of Intersal Inc., who discovered the wreck, explained that there had not been much diving around the site because of the murky water, with visibility ranging from one to ten feet. Ironically, hundreds of scuba divers had passed over the wreck, heading for other shipwrecks farther out at sea.

The NCDNCR cautiously noted that no definitive artifacts had yet been uncovered, but felt that circumstantial evidence pointed that way.

"We're not going to find anything that says *Queen Anne's Revenge*, or 'Blackbeard Was Here,'" says Wendy Welsh, manager of the state-run *Queen Anne's Revenge* Conservation Laboratory in Greenville, North Carolina. "You have to use all these little clues."

Newspaper articles, television newscasts, and Internet stories about the discovery swamped newsstands, airwaves, and the web—first in North Carolina, and eventually, all over America and around the world. For fifteen years following the discovery, the NCDNCR emphasized that the wreck was strongly thought to be the *Queen Anne's Revenge*. After a comprehensive review of the evidence, in 2011 those same officials declared that they were certain the wreck found just offshore from the small beach town of Beaufort was indeed the *QAR*, sailed by one of history's fiercest and most colorful pirates.

From the beginning of this potentially explosive discovery, all involved agreed that they did not expect "one aha moment." It would be more a process of connecting puzzle pieces. There were two main reasons for the team's certainty: the sheer size of the wreck, and the many weapons that were found in the rubble. No other ship as large as the *QAR* was known to have been in the area at the time, and a pirate ship would have been well armed, which this one was.[4]

The Rescue Begins

The company that discovered the *Queen Anne's Revenge*, although operating as a for-profit business, was well aware of the historic, cultural, and archaeological significance of this find. Within a year, they entered into a Memorandum of Agreement (MOA) with the NCDNCR,

One of the many cannons recovered from the QAR. *Conservation work is ongoing at the* Queen Anne's Revenge *Conservation Lab in Greenville, North Carolina.*
Photo Courtesy of the North Carolina Department of Natural and Cultural Resources

agreeing that the NCDNCR could keep all relics, but Intersal retained all rights to media and replica sales.

As more and more significant artifacts were recovered and brought to the surface, the state of North Carolina realized it would need a very special facility to deal with the enormity and specialization of this project. In 2004, the *Queen Anne's Revenge* Conservation Laboratory was established at East Carolina University (ECU) at Greenville, North Carolina (home of the Pirates).

By 2013, twenty-two of *QAR*'s cannons had been recovered, as well as a twelve-foot anchor weighing more than three thousand pounds. In total, as of 2018, the NCDNCR has recovered over 300,000 artifacts from Blackbeard's *Queen Anne's Revenge*.[5]

III.

THE LESSER
KNOWN

CHAPTER 9

DUNBAR DAVIS'S
LONGEST DAY

Dunbar Davis could be called the Charlie Brown of Life-Saving Service keepers. Beginning on Tuesday, August 29, 1893, fifty-year-old Keeper Davis spent fifty-five consecutive hours without sleep, food, or water while responding to five different wrecks, one after the other.

Bald Head Island and Oak Island, Then

John Dunbar Davis was born on June 30, 1843, in Smithville (renamed Southport in 1887), Brunswick County, North Carolina, several miles north and east of Oak Island. He lived there with his wife Francis Davis and their children Fanny, Catherine, Little Jack, Decatur, and three additional children unnamed in county documents. Officially, his occupation was listed as "Oak Island Life-Saving Station Captain—hero."[1] Davis was the keeper of the US Life-Saving Service Oak Island Station from 1891 to 1915. Oak Island is a small island on the extreme southern coast of North Carolina, due west of and bordering on the Cape Fear River. The one-and-a-half-story, front-gabled frame structure, built in 1889 in the characteristic Stick style of the times, had a simple but elegant look.

The chosen location of the Oak Island Station was questioned by some at the time, for a US Life-Saving Station already existed on the

The Oak Island Life-Saving Station. The station was sold to a private owner in 1938, moved directly across the road from its original location, and restored as an elegant and historic home. **Public Domain**

opposite (east) bank of the Cape Fear River, on locally named Bald Head Island (officially, "Smith Island").

"Old Baldy Lighthouse" was activated in 1818, and, learning from earlier lessons, was built farther back from the eroding shores. Today,

BRIEF HISTORY OF BALD HEAD ISLAND

Located at the mouth of the Cape Fear River, Bald Head Island ends where the treacherous sandbars known as Frying Pan Shoals begin.

In 1713, the authorities in North Carolina issued a land grant to Thomas Smith for Cape Island, which was then renamed Smith Island. Incoming sailors gave it the nickname "Bald Head," due to its large, round sand dunes. The name stuck, appearing as such on the Collet map of 1770. Everyone today calls it by that name.

"Old Baldy" Lighthouse.
Author's Photo

Old Baldy is an enormously popular tourist attraction, with annual visitation numbering around 25,000. It now holds the distinction of being North Carolina's oldest remaining lighthouse.

This was the USLSS Cape Fear Station, and Dunbar Davis was its first keeper, serving from 1881 to 1891 before being transferred to the newly established Oak Island Station. This was not only closer to home, but he wouldn't have to cross the river to get there.

The Longest Day Begins Smoothly

Almost everybody has had one of those days, either good or bad, that they will never forget. But very few (if any) of us have ever experienced anything *close* to Dunbar Davis's Longest Day. It began on Tuesday, August 29, 1893, just after the bewitching hour of midnight.

Dunbar Davis had just turned fifty years old two months prior, considered over the hill then. In those days, stations were manned by a six- to eight-person crew during the season—September through April. Stations were closed during May, June, July, and August, and the surfmen were literally sent home. The keeper and his family were still on the payroll, however, and could stay at the station, much like a dream oceanfront summer vacation.

That dream soon turned into a nightmare. In what was to become known as the Sea Islands Hurricane, a Category 3 storm rocked the coasts of Georgia and South and North Carolina. With storm surges between sixteen and thirty feet, it killed an estimated one to two thousand people with estimated damages of $1 million ($28 million in 2019 dollars).[2] Dunbar Davis would be in the middle of that storm for the next fifty-five hours, and by the time it ended, none of the following vessels were ever seen again: *Mary J. Cook, L. A. Burnham, A. R. Weeks, George W. Fenimore, Oliver H. Booth, Gertie M. Rickerson, John S. Case,* and *Lizzie May.*

Just after midnight on that Tuesday, the three-masted schooner *Three Sisters* became a victim of the tumultuous seas, with sails ripped, spars broken, and the master and mate swept overboard and drowned. The vessel then drifted helplessly off the east coast of Bald Head Island. Keeper Watts of the Cape Fear Station spotted the ship in trouble around two p.m. that day, and Keeper Davis saw it soon thereafter as well.

Although much closer to the Cape Fear Station, Dunbar Davis knew that neither station had a crew, so he headed out to assist Keeper Watts. By the time Davis got there, Watts had already rowed four miles into the storm to Southport, looking for a volunteer crew. On his way back, Watts ran into Keeper Davis. They all returned to the Oak Island Station, crossing Bald Head Island and the Cape Fear River, to get the Oak Island Station surfboat, for the Cape Fear Station was without theirs at that time. They arrived back at Cape Fear Station by one a.m. They put out the surfboat at daybreak on Wednesday, August 30, and soon reached the schooner. Despite the heavy seas, all five crew were taken off safely and transported to Southport for succor. After sixteen hours, Davis's long day was just beginning.

It Starts Getting Difficult

The day had been successful so far, but already long and tiring. Upon landing the *Three Sisters* survivors at Southport, Keeper Davis could actually see a distress flag that had been raised at his Oak Island Station. Once again, he would have to cross the island and then cross the river all alone. When he reached his station, Keeper Davis learned that the German brig, *Wustrow*, had gone to pieces nine miles west of the station. Davis immediately raised another volunteer crew, but then got word that Good Samaritan fishermen had brought all the ship's crew safely to shore. Before dismissing the volunteer crew, Davis climbed his watchtower just to double-check. What he saw startled him. The ship was closer than reported and it was fully intact; it had not gone to pieces at all. Then it dawned on him—this was a different ship! And it was in trouble as well.

This third shipwreck of the day was the 419-ton schooner *Kate E. Gifford*, and things were about to get complicated. With his volunteer crew in the surfboat, Davis pushed off, rowing toward the schooner. The hurricane-force winds were so strong that the little boat could make no forward progress. After a great struggle, they reluctantly turned back and headed for the station. "The beach was so cut through in many places," Davis reported, "that we made very slow time."

Back at the station they manned the only other means of rescue: the beach apparatus cart with the Lyle gun and breeches buoy. They began around midafternoon to pull the 2,000-plus-pound cart about ten miles through the mushy sand, violent overwash, and howling wind to reach the *Gifford*. They persisted valiantly in their lifesaving mission.

Realizing they would not reach the *Gifford* before nightfall, and seeing that the ship was still afloat, Davis decided the best use of their time was to help unload gear and cargo from the ship and attempt to remove the crew in the safety of daylight the following day. Unfortunately, the schooner crew had other plans and tried to get under way.

She ran aground instead, which complicated things. It was now sunset. It was not until two a.m. that the lifesavers were able to reach a spot opposite the schooner. The beach apparatus was set up, and a Lyle gun's projectile successfully reached the ship with a line attached. All of this was during a hurricane, at night. The men were exhausted, their muscles strained; they had had no food, water, or sleep for many hours. After all that pain and effort, there was no response from the ship. The line was taut, so it was connected, but obviously in the dark of night and with the howling winds, the ship's sailors had not seen or heard the shot (projectile).

The lifesavers could only wait. They spent an uncomfortable night on the beach.

At sunrise the next day, the connected line with the breeches buoy worked perfectly, pulling one sailor at a time safely to shore, until all seven had been rescued. While those sailors and volunteers were sent to the station, Davis and one mate stayed behind to guard the ship and cargo.

And It Continues

Keeper Davis and the mate were still keeping watch at the *Gifford* on the afternoon of Wednesday, August 30, when a small boat suddenly appeared on the horizon, coming toward them from the open ocean. Davis and the mate helped the seven men aboard get safely to shore. Davis learned that this tiny yawl was from the *Jennie E. Thomas*, waterlogged and stranded thirty-five miles offshore of the Cape Fear River. Some of the seven men were from yet another ship, the *Enchantress*, a sister ship to the *Thomas*, which had also become stranded in the same area.

Keeper Dunbar Davis had had about all he could take. He sent the seven men to his station by way of an oxen team and cart that had arrived earlier to help. This rescued yawl crew had been without food for four days. They would also get new clothes and rest at the station. The cart did not return to pick up Davis, so he spent yet another uncomfortable night on the beach.

Finally, Home!

When Keeper Davis was finally able to return to his station the following morning, he found it crowded with shipwrecked sailors—seven from the *Kate E. Gifford*, seven more from the *Jennie E. Thomas* and her sister ship, the *Enchantress*, and four from the *Wustrow*. Worse yet, all the food, clothing, and beds had been spoken for. After fifty-five hours—wet, exhausted, hungry, and thirsty—Dunbar Davis was finally home, having completed his longest day as a Life-Saver—a hero, indeed.

CHAPTER 10

AARON REPPARD

A classic example of the teamwork and persistence of the crews of the US Life-Saving Service, and a spectacular account of "America's Forgotten Heroes."

San Ciriaco, 1899

It seems like the Outer Banks's worst hurricanes happen in double-digit years—1933, 1944, 1999, 2011—but the first of the worst on record was 1899. It started in the usual manner: in the South Atlantic during the summer, long before hurricanes were named. But this one was named because it passed over Puerto Rico during the feast of San (Saint) Ciriaco, causing catastrophic damage, and would forever be known as the San Ciriaco Storm. This is the same terrible storm that set the scene for Rasmus Midgett's valiant rescue of the *Priscilla* (recounted in chapter 4).

The storm struck Hatteras Island violently on August 16. When it was over, two days later, seven vessels were lost as total wrecks on the beach; in addition, six more disappeared in the tumultuous seas without a trace.

The first known Hatteras Island victim was the *Aaron Reppard*, a three-masted, 459-ton schooner. Carrying coal from Philadelphia, Pennsylvania, to Savannah, Georgia, she had a crew of seven, with

"Awful Work of the Cyclone [Hurricane]," New York Tribune, *August 11, 1899.*
Public Domain

Captain Oskar Wessel and one very unfortunate passenger named Mr. Cummings.

Aaron Reppard departed Philadelphia on Saturday, August 12, at two p.m., towed some fifty miles down the Delaware River. For whatever reason, there she docked and remained until Monday. At five a.m., *Aaron Reppard* set sail, heading south. There was an easterly wind, uncommon there at this time of year. The winds gradually increased, and by eight p.m., they had become strong enough to warrant some battening-down procedures.

With Tuesday morning's worsening weather, a somewhat disoriented Captain Wessel reckoned he was somewhere around Cape Henry, Virginia. According to the Annual Report: "The hurricane, still sweeping northward, was furious around Cape Hatteras, while two hours prior to that time the wind was so heavy off Cape Henry, where the *Reppard* then was, that the captain hove his vessel to."[1] In sailor talk, "hove to" is the past tense of heave to, a procedure for slowing down and/or stopping a sailing ship by turning into the wind.

The Annual Report of the Operations of the United States Life-Saving Service for that year states: "[The *Aaron Reppard*] had been so strained already that the crew were kept at the pumps two-thirds of the time, and it was now too late to seek a harbor." Perhaps unaware of the full oncoming fury of San Ciriaco, or perhaps out of ignorance, *Aaron Reppard*'s captain, Oskar Wessel, decided to ride out the storm, dropping anchor offshore from Gull Shoal USLSS Station, just south of present-day Salvo. If a wooden ship can be pushed freely by hurricane winds and waves, it is relatively safe and may endure the punishment. If, however, the vessel is stationary, whether from anchorage or grounding, it becomes a target easily crushed by the huge power and force of gigantic, energy-rich waves.

"The weather was thick, rain was falling heavily, and the wind was blowing fiercely from the eastward during all the forenoon of Wednesday, and the already doomed vessel was constantly drifting shoreward, although the proximity of land was not definitely known to those on board," the Annual Report continued. Although anchored, the violent wind and waves were dragging the *Aaron Reppard* closer to shore, closer to wrecking, closer to certain doom. There was still time to hoist the anchor and be saved from crashing onto the shore.

Not only did the captain fail to do this, he in fact did the most disastrous thing possible: he ordered the sails raised. This naturally increased the speed at which the ship was being dragged to shore. Foreseeing the inevitable, all the crew and Mr. Cummings, the passenger, climbed the rigging to higher ground. The Annual Report continues, "[Sailor] Van der Graff was the last man to reach the rigging, and he says that when he got aloft, he could plainly see the shore astern, where he counted some twenty people, although he had little idea of the distance." From this perch, and already dangerously close to shore, what the ship's crew had seen were several lifesaving crews already gathered on the beach, prepared to spring into action.

The *Aaron Reppard* had been spotted by surfman William Midgett on beach patrol from Gull Shoal Station. He immediately knew that the schooner was in trouble and reported to Keeper Pugh of his Gull Shoal station upon his return. Pugh telephoned stations Chicamacomico (north neighbor) and Little Kinnakeet (south neighbor). All three stations took up positions on the beach opposite the *Aaron Reppard* with their survival equipment. The schooner was seven hundred yards offshore, out of range of the Lyle gun and in surf far too rough to launch the surfboats. The bewildered lifesavers were forced to watch helplessly as the *Aaron Reppard* dragged anchor, bouncing along the bottom, then witnessed the vessel finally run hard aground. She was now in serious trouble, and would break apart fast as the huge, angry surf pounded the wooden ship. Being stationary, the schooner was now taking the full brunt of each horrific wave. Each hit was so violent that the survivors had to literally hold on to some part of the ship for dear life.

San Ciriaco wanted to shake them off into the sea—and she soon had her way.

The *Aaron Reppard* had been dragged to within five hundred yards of the shore. This was at the limit of the reach of the Lyle gun, but worth a desperate try. The first shot burned off the line. Second shot fell short. Third shot was perfect, nearly within grasp of a crew member, but the jolting was so severe and so frequent that the sailor could not free his hands to retrieve it. The report continues, "Van der Graaf, one of the surviving sailors, says they saw the line perfectly well and knew what it meant, but that by no possible skill or courage could any of them have reached it. He declares in his testimony that if it had fallen close to him, he could have done nothing with it. 'She was pounding so heavily that it took both hands to hold on.'"[2]

The horrified lifesavers soon witnessed the mariners falling from their lofty perches. Mr. Cummings fell from the mizzenmast, caught a foot in a rope, and then became a pendulum repeatedly slamming into the mast. The mainmast snapped next, throwing its lone sailor into the deadly sea. In a panic, the captain leapt into the surf, started to swim for shore, changed his mind and turned around, and then disappeared beneath the turbulent waves.

The foremast fell next, carrying its five sailors into the sea. One was killed immediately. Another disappeared, but three others were still trying to get to shore. Seeing this, the surfmen could no longer stand by. Sworn to oath, yearning to save, but thwarted by extreme violence of wind and water, their frustration was unbearable. They formed a new plan: Members of each station began an improvisation where one would strap on a cork jacket and tie a shot line around himself while two other surfmen anchored the other end of the shot line onshore as the man with the life belt waded into the incessant, raging surf. The high winds and heavy surf carried a lethal arsenal of debris from chunks of the broken ship, including huge spars. Seventy-year-old Keeper Hooper of Station Little Kinnakeet was one of the rescuers entering the surf. Almost immediately, deadly pieces of debris struck his right leg and broke it. He continued on because he could see three sailors out there. When the lifesavers all finally emerged, they had those three sailors with them, still alive.

When a US post office arrived in the village of Chicamacomico, the name was arbitrarily changed to Rodanthe. Stubbornly resisting change, most villagers continued to use the original name. Handwritten on the photo is "Chicamacomico Burying Ground," and it's dated only weeks after the San Ciriaco hurricane.
Courtesy Outer Banks History Center

The dreadful and exhausting day had already seen failure and some successes. Yet all these men knew it was not over yet.

Lieutenant C. E. Johnston, an officer of the US Revenue Cutter Service who investigated the circumstances of this wreck, closed his report saying:

> There is no doubt that the surfmen did everything possible under the adverse conditions to save the lives of the people on this schooner. The storm was the worst in the recollection of any one now living on the Carolina Banks, and it is little short of a miracle that any one now lives to tell the tale of the wreck.

Seven ships were lost along the Outer Banks over the next two days, and six more vanished without a trace.

CHAPTER 11

EPHRAIM WILLIAMS

Cape Hatteras is famous for many things, then and now. It gave birth to several iconic mottos and monikers. The first was "The Graveyard of the Atlantic." The Ephraim Williams *story produced two more mottos.*

The Setting

Sailing is treacherous in the Graveyard of the Atlantic, especially at Cape Hatteras. Factors conspire to make vessels vulnerable to wrecking in these waters, including: the discordant directions of the Labrador Current and the Gulf Stream; the power generated when those two currents clash at Cape Point; the twenty miles of the deadly and shallow Diamond Shoals; the conflicting directions of prevailing seasonal winds; the captain's choice of saving time by going close to shore versus the safety of sailing the longer route out and around; the three hundred miles of barrier islands affording no safe port; and the big one—storms!

The Ship

The captain of the *Ephraim Williams* encountered all of these factors in December of 1884. The vessel was a 491-ton barkentine carrying a cargo of lumber leaving Savannah, Georgia, and bound for her home-port of Providence, Rhode Island. Unfortunately, she had scheduled this trip for winter, a time the US Life-Saving Service called the "storm season." Ships at this time were built from local wood and sealed with tar, the only available waterproofing material. While it is true that some wood is much better than others for this purpose, no wood is waterproof. The basic equation has always been: wood plus water equals rot. Wooden sailing ships thus had an average life span of approximately ten to twenty years.

The Disastrous Voyage

Unfortunately for the *Ephraim Williams*, the standard Outer Banks factors, plus her over-aged hull, was a recipe for disaster ready to conspire against her. On December 18, 1884, she encountered a ferocious storm off the dreaded Frying Pan Shoals. These shoals form a very large hazard to navigation created by silt and sand deposits from the Cape Fear River near Wilmington, North Carolina. The shoals extend twenty-eight miles out to sea.

The pounding of the storm had waterlogged her. She became totally unmanageable and therefore at the mercy of the winds and currents. Those same winds and currents carried her up the coast from Wilmington toward the worst place for her to be in such poor condition: Cape Hatteras. She drifted for 180 miles. She was spotted three days later, December 21, by the lifesavers on beach patrol from the US Life-Saving Service Stations of Durants (Hatteras Village), Creeds Hill (Frisco), and Cape Hatteras (Buxton). Even worse, the *Ephraim Williams*, and the Gulf Stream, had brought the storm with them. The seas were now described in the official report as "mountainous high." The captain decided to let the anchors go (drop them) in hopes of stopping the drift toward the even more dreaded Diamond Shoals, where the ship would surely break apart.

The Watch

The seas were too rough for the surfboat rescue, and the *Ephraim Williams* much too far out for the breeches buoy rescue. All the lifesavers could do was watch in frustration for the rest of the day and all through the night, "cold, wet, hungry, away from home and worried," as they later described it. They realized this also described the crew of the *Ephraim Williams*. That is, if they were still on board and alive.

The sea was as rough as it had been in recent memory. Surf was breaking as far out as a half-mile. The *Ephraim Williams* was so obscured by the breakers and the vast amount of wind-driven spray that only her masts were visible to the lifesavers onshore. As December 22 dawned, it brought changes the lifesavers didn't expect, further complicating this rescue.

The Rescue Plans

One of the most remarkable traits of the thousands of USLSS surfmen was their incredible persistence. They just never gave up.

The morning watch revealed that the *Ephraim Williams* had drifted considerably and had become stuck on Diamond Shoals, so far north as to be stranded opposite the Big Kinnakeet Station (Avon). The ship would soon be torn apart. Decisions had to be made immediately, and they would surely be life-or-death decisions.

The Big Kinnakeet crew had spent the night at the Cape Hatteras Station, the last known location of the ship, so they quickly raced back to their own station. After a quick breakfast, Station Keeper Benjamin Dailey brought up the surfboat on its horse-drawn cart. At no time during this entire saga had there been *any* sign of life from the ship. After all these hours of harsh weather, storms, and jostling, it would be easy to assume that there was no one left to save. Most of the local observers were of that opinion, and said so—but not the lifesavers. Their vigil continued.

Photograph of Keeper Benjamin Dailey in 1957.
National Park Service, Cape Hatteras National Seashore

The Miracle Begins

Around 10:30 a.m. on that Monday, a flag was suddenly raised up the masthead and joyously spotted by the anxious surfmen. Dailey immediately cried out orders that they were going out. As the surfmen donned cork life vests and gathered their equipment, one of them admitted to the keeper that he thought this was a suicide mission. Dailey dismissed him. Keeper Patrick Etheridge of Creeds Hill (Frisco) volunteered to take his place.

The Second Motto Is Born at Cape Hatteras

By 1900, Patrick Etheridge was also keeper of the Cape Hatteras Life-Saving Station (not to be confused with the lighthouse). An eyewitness at the time tells the story:

> A ship was stranded off Cape Hatteras on the Diamond Shoals, and one of the lifesaving crew reported the fact that this ship had run ashore on the dangerous shoals. The old skipper [Etheridge] gave the command to man the lifeboat, and one of the men shouted out that we might make it out to the wreck, but we would never make it back. The old skipper looked around and said, "The Blue Book says we've got to go out, and it doesn't say a damn thing about having to come back."[1]

Etheridge was not exaggerating. The *Regulations of the Life-Saving Service of 1899* stated that:

> In attempting a rescue, the keeper will select either the boat, breeches buoy, or life car, as in his judgment is best suited to effectively cope with the existing conditions. If the device first selected fails after such trial as satisfies him that no further attempt with it is feasible, he will resort to one of the others, and if that fails, then to the remaining one, and he will not desist from his efforts *until by actual trial the impossibility of effecting a rescue is demonstrated. The statement of the keeper that he did not try to use the boat because the sea or surf was too heavy will not be accepted unless attempts to launch it were actually made and failed* [emphasis added], or unless the conformation of the coast—as bluffs, precipitous banks, etc.—is such as to unquestionably preclude the use of a boat.[2]

Keeper of the Creeds Hill Station, Patrick Etheridge, whose crew assisted Dailey's Cape Hatteras LSS crew, and actually went in the surfboat as a surfman manning an oar. He had served as keeper of the Cape Hatteras Station, and is the source of the famous quote that is often mangled and even attributed to others incorrectly.
Courtesy the Outer Banks History Center

"Man the Oars!"

The entire twenty miles of Diamond Shoals is a bar. The Cape Hatteras surfmen found themselves in a thirty-six-foot-long open boat, surrounded by enormous breakers—walls of solid, powerful water sixty feet high, crashing down around them with the explosive force of mega-ton

Surfboats were manually launched directly into the turbulent surf, the most dangerous part of the ocean. This station had six surfmen and the keeper; some stations had eight surfmen. The surfmen were the oarsmen and the keeper was the coxswain.
Courtesy US Coast Guard

bombs. With no engine, the surfmen had to rely on "Arm Strong Engines"—manually rowing through five miles of massive breakers to reach the *Ephraim Williams*.

When the lifesavers' surfboat finally reached the sinking ship, they realized that if they were to pull up alongside, the violent waves would crush them and their boat. Instead, they anchored nearby, threw a line to the ship via a heaving stick, and then took the nine-man crew off one at a time. The *Ephraim Williams*'s crew had suffered December cold, hunger, and battering by the surf for *ninety hours*! Still, they had a long way to go before they slept, rowing five miles back through that awful surf. Miraculously, all made it safely.

That year, men of the US Life-Saving Service Stations, nationwide, saved 2,439 lives in peril from the sea. The nine-man crew of the *Ephraim Williams* was part of that number of lives saved by this selfless service.

The Third Motto Is Born at Cape Hatteras

The Life-Saving Service supervisor detailed to inquire into the circumstance of the gallant affair closed his report with the following remarks. Although they were meant only for bureaucrats inside the Service, they quickly resounded far and wide, and were adopted by many Coast Guard facilities as their motto:

> I do not believe that a greater act of heroism is recorded than that of Dailey and his crew on this momentous occasion. These poor, plain men, dwellers upon the lonely sands of Hatteras, took their lives in their hands and, at the most imminent risk, crossed the most tumultuous sea that any boat within the memory of living men had ever attempted on that bleak coast, and all for what? **That others might live** to see home and friends. The thought of reward or mercenary appeal never once entered their minds. Duty, their sense of obligation, and the credit of the Service compelled them to do their mighty best. The names of Benjamin B. Dailey and his comrades in this magnificent feat should never be forgotten. As long as the Life-Saving Service has the good fortune to number among its keepers and crews such men as these, no fear need ever be entertained for its good name or purposes.

For their conspicuous bravery, the boat's crew was awarded Gold Medals of the first class. Those receiving awards included Keeper Benjamin B. Dailey and surfmen Isaac L. Jennett, Thomas Gray, John H. Midgett, Jabez B. Jennett, and Charles Fulcher of the Cape Hatteras Station, and Keeper Patrick H. Etheridge of the Creeds Hill Station. During the thirty years of the Service's operation, these were seven of only twelve Gold Medals ever issued—that others might live.

CHAPTER 12

HOME

One of North Carolina's worst maritime disasters occurred on Ocracoke Island at a time before the existence of the Coast Guard or the Life-Saving Service—even before life preservers were required. This story teaches a vital lesson. (Tip: Pay attention to how many times the number "three" shows up in this story.)

There are many different types of ships and boats, each one designed and built for a specific purpose and conditions. This brings up the age-old question: "What is the difference between a ship and a boat?" There are many answers, and some are quite technical. The simplest has been spoken by sailors for years: "You can put a boat on a ship, but you can't put a ship on a boat."

As simple as that sounds, it is necessary to help understand what happened to the steam packet *Home*. Although no one would try to take an aircraft carrier over Niagara Falls, James Allaire did something almost as foolish. Allaire, an extremely wealthy New York businessman in the early 1800s, decided to flaunt his wealth by converting a riverboat to an ocean passenger liner. At the time, riverboats were prestigious and romantic and considered the best form of water transporation.

However, they were limited to river ports, and Allaire aspired to have the best of both aquatic worlds.

His conversion was fatally flawed.

The Ship

The *Home* was a 550-ton vessel, 220 feet long and 22 feet wide. She was from a new class of hybrid ships that had steam-powered side-wheel paddles but also carried traditional sails, masts, and rigging. Due to her conversions, the *Home* was a hybrid in more than one way.

These steam packets, whether on river or ocean, conjure up for us today images of the 1959–1961 TV series *Riverboat*, with Darren McGavin and Burt Reynolds, or the opulent 1951 Hollywood movie *Show Boat*, with Smithfield, North Carolina's, own Ava Gardner.

The newly outfitted *Home* was very much like those fictitious images. The interior was paneled in mahogany and cherry wood. Sparkling skylights adorned lavishly appointed passenger quarters. This was the age of wealthy folks interested in one-upmanship, and James Allaire was playing for keeps. Unfortunately, most of the upgrades were cosmetic; while passengers appreciated them, the ocean would not care in the slightest.

Bragging rights did not end with mere luxurious cosmetics. The most indisputable indication that you had reached the top echelon was to

Typical example of river paddle-wheel steamboats of the time—designed for this environment, not the ocean.
Public Domain

hold a race or set a record. And thus, those (paddle) wheels were set in motion.

Passengers who boarded the first-class *Home* were first class themselves, and only a privileged few obtained tickets. Departing from prestigious New York Harbor, they were bound for the genteel graciousness of the Old South in Charleston, South Carolina. These passengers were the upper crust of Northern industrial society, and they were used to being pampered. They had little to do but show off their wealth in extravagant ways. One male passenger made no secret of the fact that he was carrying $100,000 in cash, on his person.

There was a specific cause for all the excitement and top-notch preparations. This was only the *Home*'s third voyage. On her maiden voyage in the spring of 1837, she had set a record time from New York to Charleston. The second trip that same year had set a second record. When the third voyage was announced for October (still 1837), there was a stampede to get the limited tickets. Everyone who was anyone wanted to be part of what surely would be the new, historic record. Ninety ecstatic persons made the final passenger list to join the crew of forty-five. Unknown to them, in a fatal mistake made by shipbuilders of that era, continued until the *Titanic*, the *Home* was fitted with only three lifeboats and two life preservers, for 135 souls.

The Saturday, October 7, launch from New York Harbor was ominous. *Home* ran aground at the harbor entrance and was stuck for three hours. Once free, she began sailing south, into real trouble.

The previous month of September had seen the birth of a particularly violent hurricane starting around Jamaica. It was first observed by the British ship HMS *Racer*, and was thereafter known as Racer's Storm. The storm moved into the Gulf of Mexico, and then like a boomerang doubled back, heading for Texas, then simply followed the coast eastward until it reached Florida, crossing that peninsula and heading up the Atlantic Coast.

Racer's Storm and the *Home* were on a collision course, tragically unknown to the luxury ship's captain, Carleton White. Apparently also unknown to him and the crew was that the ship's hull had been damaged in the earlier New York grounding. If there was a riverboat gambling table on board, the deck was being stacked against the *Home*.

Three things had now combined to spell doom for the *Home*: the undetected damage from the grounding; the low ship's sides of the original riverboat design; and the increasing surf from the storm racing toward them. By the time the *Home* reached the Carolina coast on Sunday, she had already taken on ankle-deep water in her hold. Certainly, that was not much, and went largely unnoticed. And this was just the beginning. When it was eventually noticed, it would be too late.

The next morning, Monday, October 9, the *Home* began to encounter the full fury of Racer's Storm. She was now shipping water on board faster than could be pumped off. The situation had become so desperate that all the pampered passengers, including the women, were put to work, bailing with anything they could find. It wasn't enough. The *Home* was already in a serious death spiral.

Shortly before noon, October 9, 1837, Captain White saw and conceded the inevitable and formulated a new plan. A gentleman first, and then a ship's captain, he asked his passengers for permission to carry out the new plan. All agreed that changing course to beach the ship was their best chance of survival. Captain White set course for Ocracoke. Outer Banks renowned historian David Stick, in his book, *Graveyard of the Atlantic*, graphically described the situation at this point: "By this time the packet was pitching so violently that the paddle wheels were more often than not churning air, and on each wave the bow fell, independently of the stern, as much as five feet."[1]

Soon thereafter, ocean water reached the boilers, putting out the fires for the steam engines. The *Home* had no power, and now had very little hope. The few shredded sails remaining were useless. At ten p.m., the *Home* ran aground on the outer bar of Ocracoke Island. She was tantalizingly close to shore, but in these horrific conditions of violently swirling wind, water, and waves, she might as well have been one hundred miles out to sea.

At first, there were reasonably calm reactions and preparations. Women and children were herded onto the forecastle, the highest

Lithograph by Nathaniel Currier depicting the Awful Wreck of the Steam Packet *Home.*
Public Domain

part of the ship available. Then, as the inevitable disaster loomed, the understandable panic ensued. The first of the lifeboats was already lost, unloaded. The second, also empty, was crushed instantly against the side of the ship by the powerful waves as it was being lowered. The third lifeboat had successfully taken on fifteen to twenty people, from all accounts. Most tragically, however, it capsized as soon as it hit the water, and no one was seen after that.

The ship was now going to pieces. The only two life preservers were seen to be taken by two able-bodied men who jumped overboard and made it safely to shore. Then the forecastle broke, dumping the gathered women and children into the boiling surf, consuming all. At eleven p.m., only one hour after she had run aground, the *Home* broke into three pieces and then vanished.

On the third day, October 10, 1837, dawn broke to reveal a nightmarish scene—bodies of men, women, and children, with massive amounts of unrecognizable debris, littered the beach for miles. Ocracokers were somewhat used to this, and some of them gave succor to the survivors, while others helped to bury the dead. Ninety bodies—a staggering amount—were found on the beaches of Ocracoke, the largest known number of shipwreck deaths in North Carolina up until that time.

Still, there were other losses. Captain White, perhaps blamed unfairly, nevertheless lost his reputation forever. Owner James Allaire lost a very expensive uninsured boat, failed to break his cherished record, and, worst of all, lost ninety souls who had trusted his judgment.

IV.

THE ALMOST
UNKNOWN

CHAPTER 13

TIGER

The first known and documented shipwreck on the Outer Banks, the Tiger *(also spelled* Tyger*), was the flagship of England's first attempt at a North American colony. The saga of Outer Banks shipwrecks begins here—and this one changed American history.*

Sir Walter Raleigh's Lost Colony of Roanoke beginning in 1587 was the direct result of a series of falling dominoes. The first to fall, setting it all off, was a shipwreck two years earlier, less than a hundred miles to the south. Here is how it all happened.

Misinformation

The story of the Lost Colony is one of America's most famous, yet few people realize how deeply complicated this entire saga is. Popular accounts tell of colonists who settled in Roanoke and disappeared without a trace during the Anglo-Spanish War. In fact, countless traces have been discovered, including thousands of artifacts—just not on Roanoke Island.

Before we can fully understand and appreciate this, a brief background will help.

The Setting

Sir Walter Raleigh sponsored the first three English voyages to the New World in 1584, 1585, and 1587. To complete this story of the Lost Colony, we will add a fourth voyage that John White took on his own, in 1590.

This complicated story is a book unto itself, and quite a few of those have been written, so we will cut to the chase.

England was over a century behind Spain and France in approaching the New World, and in doing so risked war with these two most powerful nations in the world. Spain had already claimed all of what we know as South and Central America, plus most of western North America, the Gulf Coast, and the entire Caribbean—an incredibly vast area. France had claimed most of Canada, the St. Lawrence River valley, and much of what we now call the New England states. That left a very small target area for England—that is, if she dared.

To further reduce the risk of having war declared on England, Queen Elizabeth cleverly made this first expedition a private venture by offering a charter to business-man Walter Raleigh. These would be his expeditions, not England's (wink, wink). Nevertheless, she was heavily involved. She knighted Raleigh, loaned him a ship from her Royal Navy, the *Tiger*, as well as armaments and nine thousand pounds of gunpowder from the royal arsenal. The *Tiger* would be the flagship of Raleigh's fleet of seven vessels, and is the focus of this chapter.

Portrait of Sir Walter Raleigh, circa 1580s.
Public Domain

Original Plans for English Colony

Queen Elizabeth knew that England could not compete with Spain for New World land to exploit, as the Spanish had been looting it for nearly a century already. The Queen's plan was to put a military base on unclaimed land close to the Gulf Stream, so that English ships could raid Spanish galleons, now treasure-laden, on their way back home. That base, whose colonists were to consist of three hundred soldiers and another three hundred sailors, was to be established in 1585 at Hatteras Island (or Roanoke Island), a secluded spot between the Outer Banks and the mainland.

All of these plans would be drastically and fatally changed by a single shipwreck.

A Sixteenth-Century Sailing Primer

To reconnoiter a suitable location, Raleigh commissioned two trusted and able sea captains—Phillip Amadas and Arthur Barlow. In the late 1580s, sailing from England to North America and back home again was practically automatic. The currents of the Atlantic Ocean rotate clockwise around the rim of that great body of water. The prevailing winds do exactly the same. Basically, if a log was tossed into the ocean

THE DOLDRUMS

This term originally meant "despondency, slow, quiet, slack, sluggish, gloom, boredom," and was associated with negative images and feelings. This could describe a poor economy, a person who was depressed, or anything down and out. Sailors in the North Atlantic experienced this when their ships were stalled in the absence of wind. Since the wind currents circle the rim of the Atlantic in a clockwise fashion, the center was calm. Sailing straight across, therefore, was to be avoided. The word "Doldrums" was used specifically to identify those sluggish and gloomy maritime places.

off the coast of England, it would float south along Africa's coast, curve westward toward the northern coast of South America, then arc north into the Caribbean, pick up the Gulf Stream, "sail" past the eastern coast of North America, then continue following the Gulf Stream across the North Atlantic back to England.

To dramatically illustrate this point, a container ship lost some containers off the coast of North Carolina in a nor'easter in the winter of 2018. In May of 2019, a container full of sandals marked "Outer Banks" was found off the coast of Spain!

First: The 1584 Voyage

Recall that "a suitable spot" would be on the North American coast: It needed to be close to the Gulf Stream, north of Spanish claims, south of French claims, and provide a secret hiding place. Not an easy criterion, but remarkably, Amadas and Barlow found just such a place in the Outer Banks. This was the 1584 Expedition, departing on April 7, the first of three such expeditions known as "the Roanoke Voyages." All would be sponsored and arranged by the now-knighted Sir Walter Raleigh—soldier, sailor, statesman, man about court, businessman, and, perhaps most importantly, a favorite of Queen Elizabeth. He himself was not on board during any of these three voyages, even though it's commonly reported (erroneously) that he was.

Amadas and Barlow landed somewhere along the Outer Banks early that summer, at anchor for three days, from their original report, when the first "people of the countrey" appeared. One walked along the shore until directly in front of the English ship. Barlow then described how "the Pilot of the Admirall, Simon Ferdinando, and the Captaine Philip Amadas, my selfe, and others, rowed to the lande, whose coming this fellow attended, never making any shewe of feare, or doubt."[1]

During their short stay, the Englishmen were well received, conducting trade of valuable deerskins for copper kettles and mostly trinkets. The Englishmen were treated to feasts, were shown the extensive area of island and mainland, and were told stories. The Natives asked for

Main title page of Thomas Herriot's book. It reads as thus: "A briefe and true report of the new found land of Virginia, of the commodities and of the nature and manners of the natural inhabitants, Difcovered by the English Colony there Feayed by Sir Richard Greinuile Knight in the yeere 1585 . . ." There is more. Can you read it?
Public Domain

but were refused the "English long knives" (swords) and "fire sticks" (matchlock guns), and were asked to ally against the native enemies but were again refused.

Amazingly, two Natives, Manteo and Wanchese, agreed to sail back to England with Amadas and Barlow. The pilot of the returning ship was veteran and trusted Portuguese navigator Simon Fernando. He will be *the* key figure in the fate of the Raleigh colonies of 1585 and 1587.

The Muddied Historical Waters

Enormous amounts of confusion in the public understanding have been caused by published disinformation about the three voyages. Usually, the 1584 voyage is never mentioned. Often the 1585 and 1587 voyages are grouped together as one, or even worse, the 1587 stands alone. Here is only one example: In an excerpt from a 2011 article in the *Ocracoke Observer*, the author states a list of Ocracoke shipwrecks, but then adds, "The list does not include wreck of the *Tiger*, which took place in 1585, when Simon Fernando, chief pilot for Sir Richard Grenville's English expedition to the New World, ran aground in his flagship. Most of the gear was destroyed by the salt water, but the *Tiger* was eventually repaired and relaunched. It went on, along with the rest of the expedition, to Roanoke Island and what later became known as the Lost Colony." Again, the 1585 and 1587 colonies have been mixed up. The 1585 group was *not* the Lost Colony.

Second: The 1585 Voyage

The 1585 group was the second of Raleigh's Roanoke Voyages, but the first English attempt of a permanent colony in the New World. Here is yet another factor adding to the confusion. These people are referred to as colonists, which is correct. Most Americans, however, have implanted the image from their first-grade classrooms, conflating colonists with Pilgrims—poor men, women, and children desperately looking for freedom and a better life. This group of colonists was nothing of the sort. These were six hundred men—three hundred hardened soldiers and three hundred salty mariners, all military, and all with the singular mission of defeating their archenemy to make England wealthy, hoping to also gain fame and wealth themselves upon returning home to England.

Raleigh had only been given official Crown permission to make an English claim of land in the New World. Funding and arrangements would be strictly up to him. Wanting his success, however, Queen Elizabeth offered the help detailed above.

Raleigh then proceeded to recruit investors, sponsors, and partners. Many of the prospective deals fell through, with the proposed fleet of sixteen vessels eventually emerging as a fleet of seven. Two of these were privately owned by their captains: the 100-ton *Lion*, and the 50-ton *Elizabeth*, owned and commanded by Thomas Cavendish. The remaining four ships were owned by Raleigh. Two were substantial: the 140-ton *Roebuck*, and the 50-ton *Dorothy*. The other two were merely pinnaces (small vessels serving as tenders for the fleet).

On April 9, 1585, this fleet sailed from the famous English maritime coastal city of Portsmouth. The fleet was commanded by Sir Richard Grenville aboard the *Tiger*. The chief pilot of the expedition was

WHO'S IN CHARGE?

Commander, pilot, governor, admiral, captain.

In this maritime account of voyages and colonization, it can be confusing to determine who the boss is. The *commander* is the person in overall charge of the voyage, all ships, and all personnel, while at sea. He is the final authority with the final say. In our saga, this is Sir Richard Grenville.

The *captain* is the person in charge of one ship, a mariner and navigator (for example, Cavendish).

The *pilot* is a navigator with expertise in particular ports. To enter the port, command is temporarily turned over to him. Our pilot here is Simon Fernando.

The *governor* is the one in charge of the established colony itself, on land.

The word *admiral* at that time only meant the actual flagship in charge, not a person.

Simon Fernando. Once the voyage landed and the colony was established, the person in charge, unfortunately, was Governor Ralph Lane, by default.

The crossing was anything but uneventful, becoming a saga unto itself. Following the currents of wind and water, the fleet first went south. Almost immediately around the Canary Islands, off the west coast of Africa, the fleet ran into extremely bad weather akin to a hurricane. One of the pinnaces was sunk, the fleet was scattered, and by the time visibility was reestablished, they had lost sight of each other.

The *Tiger* proceeded on the planned course, hoping others would do the same. Fernando charted a course for a spot on the southern coast of Spanish-held Puerto Rico, where he had previously taken on freshwater. When they arrived, none of the rest of the fleet was there, forcing Grenville into this dilemma: Wait in enemy territory for the rest of the fleet, or risk going ashore for needed supplies? Most crucial was replacing the lost pinnace, which could be built from this island's forest. Incredibly, Grenville decided to anchor and send most of his crew ashore. They were ordered to first build a rudimentary fort to protect from possible Spanish attack while they built their pinnace.

The Spanish had become aware of what the English were up to, but were at reduced strength at the time, and did not challenge them. Still, the Spanish made it clear that the English were trespassing.

The English were able to build the fort and the pinnace in only eleven days, after which they eagerly set off. Right then, the *Elizabeth* appeared and joined them.

The English audacity continued. The first day out from anchor, they captured a Spanish frigate; the next day, they captured a second one. Grenville landed again shortly after, built another fort, and raided a Spanish salt mound.

Grenville set sail again, arriving in Spanish-held Isabella (now a municipality of Puerto Rico) on June 1, 1585. Amazingly, the Spanish greeted the English with a feast and serious parlaying. To encourage the English to leave, however, the Spanish offered horses, cattle, goats, swine, sheep, hides, sugar, ginger, pearls, and tobacco. It all seemed to be going the Englishmen's way!

Anchors aweigh once again.

Passing Bahama and Florida on June 23, they almost wrecked on the shoals off what they recorded as "Cape Feare." This should have been a significantly telling experience for Grenville and Fernando, but it was not a lesson completely learned. The shifting sands and shoals of North Carolina's Outer Banks likely posed navigation challenges they had rarely, if ever, experienced. It would prove the fatal downfall of the entire mission, and even significantly contribute to the failure of the *next* colony—the 1587 mission now referred to as The Lost Colony.

The First English Colony in the New World—1585

On June 26, 1585, the jubilant Grenville fleet reached its final destination. It had taken seventy-eight days to reach this inlet located between two North Carolina barrier islands. They discovered later that the Natives called this Wococon. Today, it is called Ocracoke.

Nervous over the Cape Fear near-disaster, Grenville now proceeded cautiously. For three days he lay off Wococon Inlet to fully assess the situation. Finally, he decided to enter the inlet by turning the helm over to his experienced pilot. Fernando misjudged the tricky shoals, however, and the *Tiger* ran hard aground.

Lee Miller describes the resulting scene in her excellent book, *Roanoke: Solving the Mystery of the Lost Colony*: "A heavy sea washes over the ship, driving it onto the shoal like a battering ram. Without time to recover, it is pitched hard against the bar again. And again. And again. Eighty-nine strokes in all. The *Tiger* lies exposed and helpless, repeatedly beaten, bathed in salt tears. And in this moment, unknown to John White, the fate of the [later] Lost Colony is sealed forever. From here on, all ensuing events evolve from this disaster."[2] Much of their supplies were ruined; livestock drowned, and horses swam away (possibly becoming today's famous "Ocracoke ponies"). There would not be enough food to feed the six hundred as planned, and it is far into summer, too late for planting new crops.

Consequently, only about a hundred soldiers stayed to create the colony. This would prove completely insufficient to accomplish their original directive, so they decided to extensively explore the area. This new and totally revised objective proved to be disastrous.

Miller refers to John White in 1585 as the official expedition artist of the 1585 colony. Two years later, he would become the governor of the 1587 Lost Colony.

The Ralph Lane Rampage, or Calamity Lane

The reason for the coming disaster of the Lost Colony was that the governor, Ralph Lane, was a brutal military man whose primary career in Ireland involved gleefully killing Irishmen. Lane, like many Englishmen of the time, regarded the Irish as paganistic, savage subhumans who had to be eradicated.

You can only imagine Lane's reaction to what he perceived as the even more primitive peoples he encountered here. In his bloody eleven-month stint, he and his soldiers traveled through most of what is now northeastern North Carolina, eventually reaching the Chesapeake Bay. Along the way, he burned one entire village and their crops because he

"SOM PICTVRES" FROM JOHN WHITE

White's numerous watercolor paintings of plants, animals, places, and people of the New World are stunning. They were the first images of the New World published in Europe and remained the standard for centuries.

White was aware of the predominant British feelings about the so-called savages of Ireland and the New World. With unusual sensitivity for the times, White ended his published work with "som Pictvre of the Pictes Which in the Olde tyme dyd habite one part of the great Britainne." White points out that the earliest known people to inhabit Great Britain, tribes of pagans known as Picts, were once misjudged by Roman conquerors as being primitive and savage.

A deBry 1590 engraving of White's original of a Secoton village, mainland.
Public Domain

believed one of the Natives had stolen an English silver cup. There were a number of different tribes occupying this area: Algonquin, Machapunga, Cape Fear, Roanoke, Chowanoe, Hatterask, Saponi, Weapemeac, Woccon, and Croatoan, among others. In addition, there would have been many individual villages within each tribe's territory. Lane made war on each one he encountered.

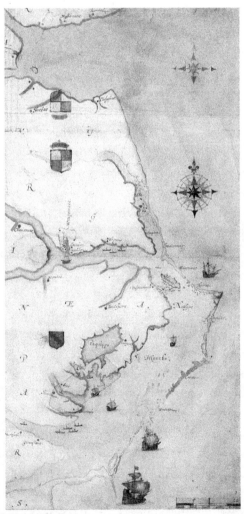

Map of North Carolina coast, drawn by John White in 1585.
Public Domain

Much Ado About Nothing

In 2012, the British Museum found something new on a John White map drawn at the time of English colonization of Roanoke. There were patches on the painting, a common "white-out" practice at the time. Under one of those patches was "a fort-like" symbol. It was located on the mainland, considerably north of Roanoke Island. Holy smoke; was *this* where the Lost Colony went to? The news went viral.

Because of his relentless hostilities, Lane knew he was in constant danger for those eleven months of travel throughout the area. This is corroborated in Paul Hulton's book, *America 1585*, where he says, "Ralph Lane's account of the colony is incomplete, but it is clear that the colonists explored and mapped the area in the vicinity of the island, in particular the Chowan and Roanoke rivers."[3] The latter is precisely where the whited-out patch on the map is located.

What most people *don't* know, however, is that in the course of his travels, Lane was "ensconcing every two days march." In simpler language, every two days' march, Lane's soldiers hastily threw up an earthen works. Hulton then tells us, "The idea of erecting a fort every two days' march was taken directly from Lane's Irish experience; it was common strategy there."[4] Affording protection they could retreat to if attacked, these amounted to little more than dirt ditches they could hide in. At the time, these were referred to as forts, although they weren't like the forts we think of today. They would be marked on period maps with "fort-like symbols." If one counts the number of "every two days" in eleven months, one finds a staggering number of English sixteenth-century "forts" scattered throughout hundreds of miles of coastal North Carolina, all of which would have left significant English artifacts from 1585, archaeologically indistinguishable from 1587.

Much ado about nothing. It was just one tiny part of Lane's rampage.

The most absurd part of this hysteria has been overlooked. The map White drew was in 1585, when it would have been impossible for him to know the location of a colony that would be built two years in the future. Furthermore, he could not have done this when he was governor in 1587, because the colonists had not left Roanoke yet.

Wingina, chief of the Roanokes, wanted to get rid of the English via a Native tribe alliance and attack. Getting wind of this, Lane had Wingina captured, shot, and beheaded. Wingina's head was gruesomely displayed on a public post—an English tradition at the time meant to graphically warn the enemy.

The Beginning of the End

By the time Lane left, all English people were obviously *persona non grata* in the New World. Back in England, Raleigh had a failure on his hands, but he still had the right to try again. This time: no soldiers, and no plans to steal gold from Spanish ships. Just men, women, and children to colonize and establish England's first land claim in the New World.

Certainly, they would not go back to Roanoke. By then the far-better port of Chesapeake had been discovered. So, more than one hundred settlers departed in 1587, bound for the Chesapeake Bay in Virginia. On the way, they planned to stop at Roanoke to pick up fifteen soldiers who had been left there previously to defend the claim, before proceeding on to Virginia.

Upon arrival at Roanoke on July 22, 1587, the pilot of this expedition, the same Simon Fernando, inexplicably refused to go on to Chesapeake, and forced all persons off on Roanoke. He undoubtedly knew this would be a death warrant for the 1587 colony. If there is any mystery to the so-called Lost Colony, this is it.

Third: The 1587 Voyage

This is another story altogether. One can see why the 1585 shipwreck at Wococon set off this series of disasters; for now, a few words about two remarkable personalities there.

Little is documented about the person and life of John White. What we do know is that he was the official artist with the 1585 colony. Father of Eleanor White Dare and grandfather of Virginia Dare, the first English child born in the New World, he was also the governor of the ill-fated 1587 Lost Colony.

Together with extraordinary mathematician Thomas Harriot, using only ground-level perspective and their eyes, they made maps of most of eastern North America and eastern North Carolina. These 400-plus year-old maps are surprisingly accurate.

One can now easily follow each of the falling dominoes: The 1585 *Tiger* shipwreck caused the lack of food and supplies, which in turn caused a drastic reduction in the number of colonists, which caused a total and drastic change in objective. This turned Ralph Lane loose on eastern North Carolina to devastate relations with the Natives, causing the second colony to change its location. It was all destined to fail from the moment that first shipwreck occurred.

Oh yes, about that 1590 voyage. This was a private adventure for John White to find his people, especially his daughter and granddaughter. When he finally did return in 1590, they were gone from Roanoke. The one clue he found was the single word CROATOAN, conspicuously carved on a post near the village entrance.

And what about those thousands of English-period artifacts that have been discovered? Many have been found on the southern end of Hatteras Island, sixty miles south of Roanoke, and more are being unearthed with each new dig. That part of Hatteras used to be joined to the northern part of Ocracoke, forming a separate island. Manteo was the son of the queen of the tribe that lived there. He thought the English were destined to be the future. His tribe was the only one not alienated by Ralph Lane. The name of his tribe and their island was Croatoan. Obviously, that is where the majority of the 1587 colonists went. They were not lost at all.

Until the fictional Lost Colony outdoor drama was written and staged in 1937, all scholarly references to it called it the "Abandoned Colony"—quite a difference.

The Controversy

It is incumbent upon us to briefly mention a long-running controversy: Scholars are still arguing—and have for years—about where the 1587 colonists went, or what happened to them. The first Dare Stone supposedly written by Eleanor Dare was found near Edenton, North Carolina, which would be north, on the way to the Chesapeake Bay. Forty-seven more stones were found stretching from there to Georgia. These latter were conclusively proven to be fakes; the first one, not so much. The most obvious problem is that they were all first found in 1937—the same year the fictitious outdoor drama was first staged.

CHAPTER 14

SARAH D. J. RAWSON

Just one of hundreds of similar unbelievable stories that rarely become known to the public, this one was uncovered and honored 112 years after the fact in a remarkable Outer Banks maritime history celebration.

The three-masted, 387-ton schooner *Sarah D. J. Rawson* left George-town, South Carolina, in February of 1905, carrying a full load of lumber to New York. It wrecked during a violent gale on February 2, 1905, off the Lookout Shoals, North Carolina. It ran hard aground at 5:30 a.m., still in the darkness of that winter morning. As soon as the schooner struck, the master gave orders to take in sail. While the crew was performing this work, a heavy sea swept the decks, carrying Jacob Hansen, a Norwegian seaman, into the raging surf, where he soon disappeared and was seen no more. The wreck was spotted by the keeper of USLSS Cape Lookout Station around noon that day.

Twenty minutes after spotting the wreck, the crew of the LSS had launched their surfboat into the treacherous breakers. The entire crew was already suffering badly from influenza, but they set out anyway, according to the book of regulations. Rowing strenuously for eighteen miles during the angry storm, with wind and heavy salt-spray lashing about them continuously, they finally reached the stranded ship. After three and a half hours of rowing and fighting the angry sea, this is what they found: "The *Rawson* lay in a seething mass of breakers, badly dismantled and surrounded by drifting wreckage, so that all efforts of the lifesavers to reach her were [in] vain. Fortunately, enough of the hull and bulwarks remained intact to afford somewhat of a shelter for her crew, 6 men."[1]

The surf was entirely too violent to come alongside without crashing into the *Rawson*. The lifesavers could see the crew, but although they repeatedly attempted to negotiate the "mine field" of lethal debris, they never got closer than two hundred yards before being driven back. Reluctantly, the lifesavers anchored their rescue boat and spent the night in the near-freezing cold, without food, freshwater, or freedom to move about. According to the annual report, "They maintained a vigilant lookout, frequently fending off fragments of wreckage that menaced their boat, until after midnight."[2] They were alone with their efforts and the vicious, wintry conditions.

About then, the temperature dropped even more, and the wind switched directions, causing them to move their surfboat about five hundred yards to an anchorage, to windward. It wasn't until 1:00 p.m. that the surf had subsided enough for the surfmen to approach the wreck. Unfortunately, it had not calmed down enough for them to actually pull alongside. Instead, they anchored again nearby and threw a line via a heaving stick. "Then one of the seamen bent (tied) the line

THE WOMEN'S NATIONAL RELIEF ASSOCIATION

First Lady Lucy Ware Hayes was the first president of the Women's National Relief Association, formed in 1880. As the *New York Times* reported at the time, the organization formed to help the USLSS, providing clothing, food, and other necessities to life-saving stations to aid shipwreck victims. The philanthropic organization honored every request for supplies from any station until the federal government began funding these supplies.

around his waist, jumped into the sea, and was hauled into the lifeboat. His companions followed his example, and, one by one, all hands were rescued—drenched, chilled, and nearly exhausted, but safe."[3] The lifesavers then covered each sailor with their own oilskin jackets and proceeded back to the station. They all arrived there at 5:30 that afternoon, safely—and utterly exhausted.

As per the standard operating procedure of the US Life-Saving Service, the survivors were furnished with food, shelter, and clothing from the Women's National Relief Association. Also, as usual, when that ran out, the lifesavers gave from their own stores. The official report concluded: "On the 12th instant the revenue cutter *Seminole* arrived in Lookout Bight, and the following day at 2 p.m. she took the crew of

The 1888 Cape Lookout Life-Saving Service Station with interesting details: Note the crew sitting at far left in summer work uniforms; the water cistern (round structure to the right); the station name and number above open boatroom doors; the beach cart at bottom of ramp, and surfboat to the right, on the four-wheel cart. The tall structure in front of surfboat is the "wreck pole" used to practice the Beach Apparatus Drill. At the extreme far right on horizon, barely seen, is the 1859 Cape Lookout Lighthouse.
Courtesy National Park Service, Cape Lookout National Seashore

the *Rawson* on board and carried them to Wilmington, NC." The *Sarah D. J. Rawson* herself then broke to pieces and completely disappeared into the violent sea.

The lifesaving crew of Cape Lookout Station bravely rescued the crew of the *Sarah D. J. Rawson*. Keeper William H. Gaskill, surfmen Kilby Guthrie, Walter M. Yeomans, Tyre Moore, John A. Guthrie, James W. Fulcher, John E. Kirkman, Calupt T. Jarvis, and former surfman Joseph L. Lewis all received the Gold Medal for extreme and heroic daring in saving the lives of others from the perils of the sea, according to the Coast Guard record. The honor never made headlines at the time, and the patriotic lifesavers later donated their medals to the war effort during World War I.

More than a century later, however, these heroes made headlines and received an additional belated honor. North Carolina congressman Walter B. Jones arranged for those medals to be duplicated and reissued to the lifesavers' descendants. Authentic to the originals, each medal was inscribed with the surfman's name, number, and a description of the rescue. The heroes of the *Sarah D. J. Rawson* rescue were posthumously honored at a grand ceremony in 2017, keeping their legacy alive for the next generation.

CHAPTER 15

THE WRIGHT BROTHERS AND THE US LIFE-SAVING SERVICE

Pursued for thousands of years, the secrets that made manned flight possible were finally and triumphantly discovered by two bicycle mechanics from Dayton, Ohio, Wilbur and Orville Wright. But those secrets were not revealed on the famous date of December 17, 1903. And the place was nearby, but not in Kitty Hawk, North Carolina. The Wrights had a secret weapon, one of the least-known stories in all of American history. They are America's forgotten heroes. Here is that incredible story, and why it may have been suppressed.

A Complicated Story Commonly Oversimplified

The Wright brothers' story has much more to it than most of us know, and is often grossly oversimplified. We have all heard the version we tell to six-year-olds so many times that we now take it as simple truth: Two brothers from Dayton, Ohio (and they always put Orville first and then Wilbur, when it should always be the other way around), were interested in trying to fly. Although they were only bicycle mechanics, they worked very hard. They came to Kitty Hawk on the North Carolina Outer Banks in 1903 to test their experiments, and on December 17, became the first people in the world to fly!

Truth? Most of it. Simple? No. Much is left out and glossed over, which can lead to huge misunderstandings. That is why we still hear of others claiming to have flown before the Wright brothers. (This will be clarified later.) To fully understand and appreciate this information about their little-known secret factor, the story must be put into context.

The Context

It begins with the realization that the very earliest humans copied the behavior of animals they saw. These people could eventually run like a gazelle, climb like a monkey, crawl like a snake, and swim like a fish . . . But they never could *fly* like a bird. Surely they tried in vain many, many times.

Thousands of years ago, the ancient Greeks had Icarus in their mythology and Pegasus in their legends. Italy's Leonardo da Vinci invented a helicopter—on paper. Persian legend had King Kaj Ka'us attaching eagles to his throne so he could fly around his kingdom. Alexander the Great had a similar legend, only with griffins. Although these are all myths and legends, they clearly document very early interests in the possibility and desire for controlled manned flight.

Actual flights manipulated by man began with Chinese kites around 400 BC. Over two thousand years later, France's Joseph and Jacques Montgolfier invented the first passenger hot-air balloon. Man flew! Gliders showed up in the early 1800s, most of them with disastrous results, although they flew for a while. Germany's Otto Lilienthal was the first to almost master glider flights in 1891. His machine looked much like today's hang-gliders. He made over 2,500 glides before he crashed and was killed. This single incident had a profound effect on Wilbur Wright, triggering what was to become an unquenchable desire to discover what went wrong. Thus, Wilbur's start (Orville was not to be involved for some time) was with the book Lilienthal had written. This became the basis of Wilbur's initial designs.

The Industrial Age of Inventions

Now it's going to get complicated! The late 1800s and early 1900s saw a flurry of aeronautical experiments and activity. Flight was also the topic of many daily conversations, scientific debates, professional magazine articles, and scholarly speeches. The world was clearly polarized into two camps: those who believed that manned flight was not only possible, but also imminent and desirable; and those who passionately believed that it was not only impossible, but also the crazy talk of cranks (interestingly, a word Wilbur used in a letter to the Smithsonian) and, worst yet, blasphemous. Perhaps the biggest irony in this entire story is that the author of the now-famous phrase, "If man was meant to fly, God would have given him wings," was Wilbur and Orville's father, Bishop Milton Wright.

By the late 1800s, there was a great deal of new activity going on all over the world. It was a continuation of the wondrous Gilded Age, really, the Age of Inventions, starting in the 1870s. It was the beginning of the transcontinental railroad, the telephone, electricity, Standard Oil, steel, the Kodak camera and roll film, the automobile, the gasoline engine, radio, tape recorders, elevators, air-conditioning, and, in the same year as their first manned flight, 1903, the EKG (electrocardiogram), among many other inventions worldwide.

Modern Aviation Pioneers

Many men designed and built flying machines. Some were powered, usually by steam, and some were not. A few of the more-serious inventors were American-born Brit Sir Hiram Maxim, in 1894; Augustus Herring from Georgia, in 1896; the Texas Baptist minister and sawmill operator, Reverend Burrell Cannon, in 1900; Gustave Whitehead, born in Germany but then a Connecticut resident, in 1901; and in 1903, Karl Jatho of Germany and Richard Pearce of New Zealand. But even if these men flew, and could prove it, that was *not* what the Wright brothers were claiming to have been the first to accomplish. It was something far more significant. (More on that later, for this is the biggest popular misconception.)

In fact, the Wright brothers actually worked with some of their rivals, some even in their Kill Devil Hills camp, including Edward Huffaker, George Spratt, and Octave Chanute. They relied on the latter in the beginning, as their mentor. Chanute had done a lot of work early on, and was considered the world's leading authority on aerodynamics at the time, but had "retired" due to age. Still, he was delighted to help the Wrights, and often said they were ahead of him in terms of discovering more aero details than he had.

Langley

The most serious challenge to the Wright brothers, however, was very real, and it came from a very respectable source: Samuel Pierpont Langley. Then secretary of the Smithsonian Institute in Washington, DC, Langley's personal involvement with flying-machine research started in 1887, and became obsessive by the early 1900s. By 1903, Langley had been working on the project for sixteen years, had the entire staff of the Smithsonian and all of its resources at his disposal, and received a $50,000 grant ($1 million today) from the US War Department, initiated directly by President McKinley himself. In spite of all this, Langley's attempts were all dismal failures. His sixth and final failure was on December 8, 1903—just *nine days* before the Wrights' success. (The brothers achieved their victory after only two tries, in just three days!) Langley was ridiculed nationally.

On the Wright Track

It was in this kind of high-pressure and high-profile environment that Wilbur and Orville began to operate in 1900. Wilbur specifically wanted to avoid the spotlight or any advance publicity. Unlike Langley with his many advantages, the Wrights performed all of their experiments at their own expense and on their own time. Their staff included the two of them; shop mechanic Charlie Taylor, who built the flyer's engine; and the Wrights' younger sister Katharine. She covered the shop in their absence and recorded and saved their correspondence.

Wilbur's first, best idea was what he called *wing-warping*. The idea was to bend one wing tip one way while bending the other tip the opposite way. He observed this while watching gliding birds turn in flight. He tested this idea on a large box kite he flew in Dayton in 1899. It worked! This would be a *major key* to their eventual success, but it is still not the secret factor. That part of the story—about wing warping—has been well told.

Kitty Hawk

Off to Kitty Hawk! Orville finally becomes involved. The Wrights' experiments there in 1900 were mildly successful, although they discovered that some obvious improvements were needed. When those improvements were implemented in the next season, in 1901, they were a disastrous failure. Wilbur even sarcastically remarked that the plane flew better backwards.

They had now moved their camp to the base of a natural geographical area the locals called the Kill Devil sand dunes. This was four miles south of the village of Kitty Hawk, from which they were launching their glider. They had done their homework and had followed all the rules. It made no sense to a disgusted Wilbur, who seemed ready to give up. On the train ride back to Dayton, he said to brother Orville, "Not within a thousand years would man ever fly." The number "one thousand" proved to be prophetic, but not as Wilbur had thought. It would be part of the secret factor.

Knowing the pressure and the competition, and realizing that they had failed because they'd followed the rules, Wilbur reasoned that the rules must be wrong.

After new figuring in the off-season, it turned out that the rules of lift were indeed wrong. Wilbur recalculated the existing air pressure tables and made substantial other improvements before the brothers returned once more to their Kill Devil Hills camp, now with greatly renewed optimism and enthusiasm.

From his extensive bicycle experience, which included high-speed racing, Wilbur had an advantage of perspective that none of his competitors had: He knew that the bicycle, like the airplane, is an inherently unstable machine. Any three-year-old can hop on a tricycle and master it the first time, because that machine is stable. But we all remember our many first tricky attempts at riding a bicycle without the stabilizing training wheels.

The brothers realized that to master the airplane, like the bicycle, the operator would need a great deal of knowledge. Most importantly, with something so new that operated in three dimensions, like nothing else before, it would require extensive practice. All previous transportation methods occurred in two dimensions: walking, horseback riding, wagons, and cars—you go forward, backward, or left or right. But once in the air, the plane also goes up and down. Wilbur had made a speech in Chicago to the Western Society of Engineers as early as 1901 where he said, "A thousand glides is equivalent to about four hours of steady practice. This is far too little to give anyone a complete mastery of the art of flying . . . The soaring problem is apparently not so much one of better wings as of better operators."[1]

The Secret Factor Revealed

This, then, leads directly to the secret factor of their 1903 success. Wilbur's interest in moving their camp to the base of the Kill Devil sand dunes was for several good reasons.

The four hills provided different heights for launching the glider; soft sand for landings; and the lack of prying eyes. By then, however, Wilbur had discovered a *monumental* reason for relocating there: A station of the US Life-Saving Service was there on the beach—the Kill Devil Hills Station.

A young, hardy crew of surfmen was stationed there, along with the keeper. This would be an important and ready source of labor and other

WHY THE ODD NAME OF "KILL DEVIL HILLS"?

A particularly bad rum produced in the area was laced with extremely hot peppers to hide the awful taste. The word *rum* is first recorded in 1654 in the Public Records of the Colony of Connecticut, where it is mentioned along with another of its names, "kill devil." The terrible liquor produced in this part of North Carolina therefore lent its name to the place.

The area in question was a group of large, natural sand dunes that the locals called Kill Devil Dunes. They were located about four miles south of the remote village of Kitty Hawk, on the Outer Banks of North Carolina.

Early rums of the period were commonly referred to as "kill devil," but sources do not agree on the term's origin. In the food world, *devil* means "spiced," and Old English cooking techniques often employed a kiln as opposed to an oven. *Kiln-deviled* could have been a reference to "cooked with spice," easily mistranslated to the common "kill devil" liquor.

assistance. Due to the extreme isolation, there were no other people for miles around. The closest village was Kitty Hawk, with a population of only three hundred. With the help of these "indispensable men" (title of a Coast Guard publication), the Wrights completed around one thousand glides that season.

What did this extensive practice and experience teach them? They learned how to control an aircraft in the air: They could make it go up and down (pitch), make it turn from right to left (yaw), and best of all, how to bank into a turn (roll), just like a racing bicycle would do! The NASA website says of the 1902 experience, "For the first time in history, a craft could be controlled in three dimensions."

Therefore, all previous claims of "I flew before the Wright brothers" are meaningless. Although the Wrights didn't claim to be the first to fly, they were the first to control an airplane in flight in a heavier-than-air machine operated by a pilot, turning and landing the machine exactly as they wished. No previous claim could match that.

The 1878 Kill Devil Hills Life-Saving Station, with crew that assisted the Wright brothers.
Courtesy National Park Service, Cape Hatteras National Seashore

Flying only? An arrow flies. A baseball flies. A kite flies. A car can fly if it is driven over a cliff. But none of those are controlled. None of those can go up as well as down once in flight. All of them start at a higher point than they land. None of those can land exactly where they want to. None of those had the potential to carry cargo, or even—dare we say it—passengers. All of those characteristics apply to Whitehead, Maxim, Herring, Jatho, Cannon, Pearce, Spratt, Huffaker, Chanute, or Langley. Or anyone else. In short, *none* of those did any practical good. The Wrights did. And who of this group continued to fly in public after their initial claim? *Only* Wilbur and Orville!

Extensive practice with the 1902 glider in the Kill Devil Dunes. Wilbur did all of the flying in 1901 and 1902. Again, surfmen from the Kill Devil Hills Life-Saving Station are assisting, in partial dress uniforms.
Courtesy National Park Service, Wright Brothers National Memorial

It was on the Kill Devil Dunes with the 1902 glider, then, that the secrets of manned, controlled flight were learned for the first time in human history. This is what Wilbur was looking for from the absolute beginning. Realizing the extreme significance of that brilliant find, Wilbur applied for and received a United States patent. That patent was for the 1902 glider, not the much more famous 1903 powered plane.

What Wilbur received from the US Patent Office was actually a patent on controlled flight: Every fixed wing plane that would successfully fly from that point on was using Wilbur's patent, including today's space shuttle. Wilbur took each violating company to court and won every case. This became very stressful, however, and it taxed Wilbur's mind and body. In 1912, at only forty-two years old, he contracted typhoid fever, and due to his weakened state, never recovered. He died on Thursday, May 30. On the other hand, Orville lived until 1948, which accounts for him being better known.

Many factors contributed to the Wright brothers' success, including the number of aerial experiments going on at the time, all over this country and in parts of Europe, amid stiff competition. The numerous successful glides throughout 1902 provided invaluable experience, helping the Wright brothers to learn what they needed to know. The specs on the 1902 bi-wing glider were on point, with a wing span of thirty-two feet; a length of sixteen feet, one inch; a height of eight feet; and a weight of only 117 pounds. The enormous sand dunes stood as high as one hundred feet and had no grass or vegetation.

The saving grace, though, was the life-saving crew of strong young men located just yards away who had time to help and were always at the ready. Members of this crew toted that glider up the hills a thousand times in 1902. This was the largely untold secret factor. Wilbur himself had already indicated that their success never would have been possible without this kind of extensive practice.

Could Wilbur and Orville have made one thousand glides if they'd had to carry the glider uphill each time by themselves during their short stays?

The 1903 flying machine. Interesting details in this shot: The plane is placed on the monorail on the Big Kill Devil Dune where Wilbur first tried unsuccessfully on December 14. The four lifesavers are wearing their dress uniforms, which is not what they worked in; this is specifically for this photo, which Orville took. Notice the two boys and their dog. Confusing to modern eyes, the plane is facing us, to go down the rail to the left. The rudder is made up of the two "wings" in the front, to control pitch, or up and down. "Pusher propellers" are in the back. Also notice the total absence of grass or vegetation.
Courtesy National Park Service, Wright Brothers National Memorial

To dramatically illustrate that point for yourself, the following challenge is issued: Get a partner; find a 117-pound weight that you both can carry; go to Jockey's Ridge State Park, Nags Head, North Carolina (very similar to what Big Kill Devil Hill was like in 1903—all sand, and only six miles south of the actual Kill Devil Hills site).

Now climb the steepest face of one hundred feet of that dune carrying your 117-pound weight. In suits and ties. With leather shoes. Oh, but wait! It's not just the weight you have to deal with. There is also the bulk and unwieldiness of the object (sixteen feet long and eight feet high). But there's more. It also has two wings, thirty-two feet across, which produce lift when air passes over them, and there is always a breeze on the Outer Banks, so this awkward 117-pound object is constantly being jerked out of your grip. Finally made it to the top? Great; now just 124 more times today. Then get some rest. You need to do it another 125 times tomorrow. That only represents two days in October, full of gusty autumn winds. You will need to do it another 750 times in sixty days to duplicate the 1902 experience.

THE KITTY HAWK VS. KILL DEVIL HILLS CONFUSION

Two factors account for this confusion: geography and time. The only nearby village was Kitty Hawk, whereas the flights took place at a geographical region of large dunes known as the Kill Devil Hills four miles to the south. The modern town of Kill Devil Hills was not incorporated until 1953. The closest telegraph office to the brothers' camp was the US Weather Bureau in Kitty Hawk. So, on the afternoon of December 17, 1903, after their four successful flights, Wilbur and Orville happily walked the four miles to the Kitty Hawk Weather Bureau Station. Their telegram, of course, would be imprinted as coming from Kitty Hawk, NC, and that name would forever be connected to that historic event. Much of that original Kitty Hawk LSS Station nearby has been incorporated into the Black Pelican Oceanfront Restaurant, still located in Kitty Hawk today.

Does anyone really think Wilbur and Orville did all of this by themselves? Obviously, it was the men of the Kill Devil Hills Life-Saving Service Station. The Wright brothers and the US Life-Saving Service: America's genius and America's heroes worked very well together.

So why is this part of the story so little known? Because the USLSS surfmen were federal employees significantly assisting the Wrights' success, and the failed, high-profile Samuel Langley had also been federally supported.

V.

THE MYSTERIOUS

CHAPTER 16

CARROLL A. DEERING

The five-masted schooner that wrecked at Cape Hatteras on January 31, 1921, is called the "Ghost Ship of the Outer Banks" for good reason. She was discovered run hard aground on the Diamond Shoals. Sails were set, food had been served at the table, and everything was in place—except for the fact that the lifeboats and critical navigation aids were missing. No one on board. Even after the extensive Coast Guard search and investigation that followed, they found no answers. With so much written about this event, and with so few actual facts to go on, there is little we can do here but relay the basic details. As with any mystery, it is up to you to wonder and ponder. But we have added a twist!

Headlines and Opening Lines

There have been hundreds of articles, accounts, and writings about this wreck, and they all start in a similar way. Here are a few examples:

> To this day, the *Carroll A. Deering* is one of the most discussed and written-about maritime mysteries of the twentieth century, its enduring popularity no doubt fueled by the complete uncertainty as to how the ship arrived at its fate.[1]

> One of the most written-about ghost ships in history.[2]

MARY CELESTE

An earlier story, about the 282-ton brigantine *Mary Celeste*, is eerily similar to the story of the *Carroll A. Deering*. It too was discovered as a ghost ship. The *Mary Celeste* had departed New York Harbor on November 7, 1872, bound for Genoa, Italy, with a huge cargo of 1,701 barrels of industrial alcohol. Almost a month later, on December 5, she was spotted adrift, four hundred miles east of the Azores. The captain, his wife, their two-year-old daughter, a crew of eight, and the vessel's single lifeboat were missing. The ship was in good shape. Their fate remains unknown, creating another nautical mystery.

> The *Deering* is one of the most baffling mysteries in maritime history.[3]

> Abandoned and deserted, with all of its eleven crewmen missing, the circumstances are as strange as those of the *Mary Celeste*, and her demise remains as one of the greatest unsolved maritime mysteries of all time.[4]

The Ship

The *Carroll A. Deering* was a 1,879-ton, five-masted schooner built by the G. G. Deering Company at their shipyards in Bath, Maine, completed in 1919. Owner Gardiner Deering named the ship for his youngest son, Carroll Atwood Deering, bookkeeper for the company.

There were several unusual things about this ship right from the start. It was the last of exactly one hundred ships constructed by the Deering Company. It was also one of the last commercial wooden sailing ships to be built anywhere in the world, as the age of steel and steam was dawning and rapidly expanding, clearly the way of the future.

The *Deering* was unusual for its time. According to an article written by Ian Harvey, "She was 255 feet long and 45 feet wide, with 5 masts and 3 decks. She was luxurious for a cargo ship, outfitted in oak, mahogany, and ash wood, with a functioning lavatory, steam heat, and electricity."[5]

Launched into the Kennebec River of Bath, Maine, on April 4, 1919, she was to be captained by Gardiner Deering's friend and neighbor, William Merritt. Known as "Hungry Bill" to his nautical acquaintances, Merritt was also a hero of the Great War. He took the *Deering* out almost immediately on her maiden voyage, from Newport News, Virginia, to Rio de Janeiro, with a full load of coal. The return trip was bound for New York with a cargo of Argentine corn. She made two more voyages in 1920, both from US East Coast ports to the Caribbean. In only three trips, the *Deering* had already recovered half of her construction costs.

The Final Voyage Sails

The yearling *Deering*'s next voyage was scheduled to once again depart from Norfolk, Virginia, bound for Rio de Janeiro, this time with another load of coal which had been delivered from West Virginia to Norfolk by train. This would be an arduous trip of 4,644 statute miles (4,048 nautical miles) through some famously treacherous—and mysterious— waters, as well as some demanding climates. There were risks, certainly, but every captain was aware of this on every voyage. Many of these old salts considered such difficulties a professional and personal challenge. Besides, the *Deering* had made this voyage several times already.

Changes for the Worse

Captain Merritt was also a sizable part owner of the ship, giving him the privilege of selecting his twenty-nine-year-old son, Sewall Merritt, as his first mate. The schooner set sail from Newport News, Virginia (near Norfolk), on Sunday, August 22, 1920. Soon thereafter, Captain Merritt fell seriously ill. He tried to hang on for the next five days, but his condition worsened.

The ship was hastily docked in **Lewes, Delaware,** so the captain could depart the vessel. Accompanied by his son, he sought immediate medical attention. It was decided he should not continue sailing but stay in Lewes to recuperate. The Deering Company was notified and began scrambling for a substitute captain. Merritt suggested his friend and neighbor in Portland, sixty-six-year-old retired captain Willis B. Wormell. The new first mate, Charles B. McLellan, a mysterious figure himself, would become the central character in the remaining part of this mystery. It remains unclear how and why he was selected.

There was another negative change. The reliable crew previously assigned to this voyage refused to sign on because the port in Rio had no cranes with which to unload the coal. Consequently, it was to be a hot, dirty, painful, and labor-intensive job done by hand, with crewmen going down into the hold. The new bos'n was Fredrickson, from Finland. Inexplicably, Finns were considered nautical bad luck. The rest of the crew were all Danes. The entire complexion of the ship had now changed, and not for the better.

Under this new leadership and personnel, the *Deering* departed Delaware on Wednesday, September 8, 1920. At least it wasn't Friday, a day on which Christian mariners never set sail, due to Christ's crucifixion. Although most reports say that the outbound voyage was uneventful, questionable incidents that followed indicate there were already undisclosed problems about to bubble to the surface.

First Open Signs of Trouble

After docking in Rio, Wormell gave his crew shore leave. While there, Wormell ran into an old friend, Captain George A. Goodwin, who, ironically, was from the Maine town of Lubec, where Wormell was born. Wormell felt free to express his now-serious concerns about the entire personnel situation aboard the *Deering*. "I have a worthless mate," he said. "Second mate not much better,"[6] Bland Simpson records in his book, *Ghost Ship of Diamond Shoals.* Wormell also said that his first mate was a bad man and a troublemaker. Wormell stated that McLellan

Captain Jacobson of the Cape Lookout Lightship was the last to see the Carroll A. Deering *before the wreck.*
Courtesy National Park Service, Cape Lookout National Seashore

had obvious disdain for his captain, which blew up dramatically and publicly soon after this conversation. When Goodwin brought up the uneasy prospect of mutiny, Wormell admitted that it had crossed his mind.

Unfurling her sails and casting off, *Carroll A. Deering* departed Rio on Thursday, December 2, 1920. Wormell charted her course for the return journey home. Unfortunately, she had no cargo. On Christmas day, Mrs. Wormell heard from her husband that he was on his way home, "with the most unruly crew ever."[7] The first stop for supplies was Barbados, where the crew went ashore. McLellan went to the

Continental Café, whereupon he proceeded to get drunk, loud, boisterous—and threatening. He told another ship's captain, Norton, and the captain's first mate, that Wormell was a bad captain. Furthermore, he stated that he, McLellan, had to do all the navigating due to Wormell's poor eyesight. McLellan complained that Wormell not only failed to properly discipline his crew, but that he also interfered with McLellan when he tried to control the crew. Most damaging, Captain Norton and his aides heard McLellan say that he would kill Captain Wormell before the end of the voyage. The disorderly McLellan was arrested on the spot and put in jail. Remarkably, Captain Wormell went out of his way to get McLellan released. It is not known why.

The Nightmare Begins: A Timeline

The negative atmosphere from Barbados continued to haunt the return voyage.

Sunday, January 23, 1921: Until this date, Captain Wormell's handwritten notes were on the ship's map. After this date, a different handwriting is the only one that appears.

Saturday, January 29, 1921: Six days later, the *Deering* is spotted by Captain Jacobson of the Cape Lookout Shoals Lightship 80. Jacobson reported that a crewman with red hair and a foreign accent hailed him saying that the *Deering* had lost her anchors and needed to be reported to the parent company. Jacobson further notated that the shouting man did not look like a captain or a first mate, the only ones who could properly deliver such a distress message. He further noted that other crew members were gathering on the foredeck of the ship, strictly forbidden by maritime traditions of the time. None of this was normal. Worse, it was the last time anyone saw the *Deering* at sail with her crew.

Later that day, Jacobson reported a steamer passing by his lightship. He noted that it had no visible name. He sent a signal for it to stop, but the ship steamed on, following in the same direction the *Deering* had gone. Again, this was out of the norm.

THE DIAMOND SHOALS

Merriam-Webster defines *shoals* simply as "1: shallow; 2: a sandbank or sandbar that makes the water shallow." Think of shoals as a large group of underwater sand dunes and/or sandbars that are not only shallow, but constantly shifting with every passing wave, making them "unchartable." Chapter 2 explains how the Diamond Shoals were formed.

Monday, January 31, 1921: On regular beach patrol from the US Coast Guard Station 183, Station Cape Hatteras, at 0530 hours, surfman C. P. Brady spotted the schooner *Carroll A. Deering* immobile on the Diamond Shoals. According to an original report provided by the Outer Banks History Center, "The schooner was driven high up on the shoals in a boiling bed of breakers."

Friday, February 4, 1921: Due to the severity of the storm and the resulting tumultuous seas, it took another four days for the Coast Guard to reach the stranded *Carroll A. Deering*.

Official 1921 US Coast Guard photo of the crew at Station Cape Hatteras who responded to the wreck of the ghost ship Carroll A. Deering.
Outer Banks History Center, North Carolina Department of Cultural Resources

This Is What They Found

Almost every one of the hundreds of articles written about this amazing story includes these details: The ship was still under full sail. And there was no living thing on board except for a single six-toed cat.

Prepared food was found in the galley, indicating a very sudden departure. The two lifeboats were missing. Also critically missing were all the documents, charts, navigational instruments, and the chronometer. Whoever took these knew what they were doing, for these items were crucial for navigating anywhere, but especially in the Outer Bank's Graveyard of the Atlantic. It was confirmed that the anchors were indeed missing, as reported earlier at Cape Lookout.

Further details that might have a bearing on the mystery were that red light distress signals had been sent up the mast. Inspection of the captain's cabin revealed a spare bed having recently been slept in and three pairs of boots that were left behind. Finally, Captain Wormell's handwritten log entries on the ship's map were replaced with another hand after January 23.

In the following months, thorough investigations were conducted by the US Coast Guard, the Federal Bureau of Investigation, the US Navy, and the official US Departments of State and Justice. No conclusive

POLYDACTYL CAT FACTS

The facts about this six-toed cat are unclear and at times contradictory. While some reports say there were several cats on board, most say there was just one. It has been described as a gray cat or a yellow cat. It has been reported that the locals had first looted the ship and brought back the cat. Also reported was that the Coast Guard took the cat off. Today, there are a number of six-toed cats in Hatteras Village that hang around the Burrus Market and the fishing docks. Perhaps they are somehow descended from the cat that came from the wreck of the *Carroll A. Deering*? A mysterious subplot.

answer was ever determined. The Coast Guard investigation alone was the most extensive it had ever done up to that time.

The Predominant Theories

It is inevitable—and unpreventable—to try to solve a mystery; it's part of human nature. The appeal of a mystery is that it challenges the intellect to investigate and connect clues in an effort to come to a logical conclusion. An even more primordial appeal is that since no one else really knows the answer, yours can be just as good as any other. Consequently, theories abound on the mystery of the *Carroll A. Deering*.

The following are the most commonly accepted.

Mutiny is considered the best theory because so much hard evidence points to it. Clearly there was open animosity between the two authority figures, Captain Wormell and First Mate McLellan. The hostility was both personal and professional: Neither liked the other personally, and professionally, they had opposite views on running a ship and managing its crew. Most damning, of course, was McLellan's drunken tirade about killing Captain Wormell.

The fact that Wormell's handwriting was replaced by that of an unknown person from January 21 to January 23 is extremely indicting. It does not necessarily prove that he was killed and thrown overboard, but possibly that he was incapacitated or restrained.

What does not support this theory are these facts: If McLellan had committed murder or instigated a mutiny, he had seriously transgressed the law, meaning he would want to run and hide. So, why did the *Deering* alert the lightship that they had no anchors? Why create a written record by requesting that the Deering Company be informed? Why would the red distress lights have been run up the mast to signal for help? Why would Wormell have had McLellan released from jail? The answers to most of these questions are obvious, thereby clearly indicating that this theory has flaws.

One of the most alluring theories centers around pirates. With the Blackbeard heritage and the pirate theme enormously popular with Outer Banks tourists today, this is a natural fit.

There is specific evidence that during a police raid on a Communist Party headquarters in New York, papers were found calling on Communist Party workers to seize American ships and sail them to Russia. In April of 1920, a German fishing schooner, the *Senator Schroeder*, was captured by Russian pirates and sailed to their home. In June of 1921, there was widespread panic in Paris as reports started coming in of large numbers of ships and crews disappearing in European waters. These and similar incidents and reports thus created an atmosphere where piracy was considered a likely cause of the *Deering* mystery. The obvious problem with this theory, however, is that the ship was not stolen, but abandoned. A modern luxurious and huge workhorse hauler such as the *Carroll A. Deering* would have been an extremely coveted prize for pirates, which they would have gleefully captured and used.

A hurricane is another likely theory, as the number-one cause of thousands of shipwrecks over the centuries in the Graveyard of the Atlantic has been storms. It is on record that there were hurricane winds reported by Lightship 80 on January 27, 1921. The US Weather Bureau cited that nine other ships had disappeared or been damaged in that area at the same time.

One school of thought that would disprove this theory is that by January 31, the storm had passed. This landlubber view, however, only recognizes wind speed. As any mariner—or coastal resident of the Outer Banks—knows, hurricane winds whip up gigantic waves in the ocean which persist in size and danger long after the winds have subsided. The *Deering* and the other nine ships most likely were still experiencing these highly destructive circumstances. This will be pursued further with our new theory, presented below.

An intriguing subcategory of the storm theory here: It is known that another ship, the steamer SS *Hewitt*, was close to the *Carroll A. Deering* at this time. Some even speculate that this was the unnamed mystery ship that passed Cape Lookout without stopping and continued in the same path behind the *Deering*. The plausible argument was that the *Deering* crew abandoned ship and the nearby *Hewitt* picked them all up, but shortly thereafter sank in the storm, taking all traces of the

Deering crew with her. The abandoned lifeboats would also have been carried far away, to eventually sink.

The least likely—but understandably popular—theory is that the *Deering* was captured by rumrunners. Once again, the atmosphere of the era is conducive to this theory, as this was during Prohibition (1920–1933). Although the Eighteenth Amendment to the US Constitution prohibited "the manufacture, sale, or transportation of intoxicating liquors within, the importation thereof into, or the exportation thereof from the United States," it did not prohibit possession or consumption of alcohol. It's widely believed that Americans drank more alcohol during Prohibition than before or after.

Rum-running became a large and profitable business during this period, with rumrunners shipping in alcohol that was legally produced in Mexico, Europe, Canada, and the Caribbean. And as we know, the *Carroll A. Deering* was returning to a "dry" America from the "wet" Caribbean. This all fits neatly into a theory, except for two things that don't make sense. First: Why capture a slow-moving sailing ship when faster steamships were all around? And second: Even if captured, why abandon it? Why dispose of the crew? Murder is a much more serious and harshly punished crime than theft.

Final Known Facts

The Coast Guard cutter USCGC *Manning* attempted to salvage the *Deering* by towing her off the Diamond Shoals. For a number of reasons, the difficult circumstances made this impossible. Due to its charged missions, by remaining on the Diamond Shoals, the *Carroll A. Deering* would be "a hazard to navigation." So, on March 4, out of pure frustration, the Coast Guard dynamited the ship. Much of it was dispersed over a wide area. One of the largest pieces eventually washed ashore on Ocracoke Island, but was later removed by a hurricane. On the Outer Banks, as Dorothy from the *Wizard of Oz* said, "People [and things] come and go so quickly here!"

What Really Happened to the *Carroll A. Deering*— My New Theory

On January 30, 1921, the schooner *Carroll A. Deering* had just passed through a violent hurricane that had already wrecked dozens of ships near Cape Hatteras. Suddenly, the sailor on watch spotted what appeared to be a leftover mine from World War I, which had ended just three years earlier. It was widely known that German submarines had placed extensive mine fields all along the US East Coast, especially around the Wimble Shoals off Chicamacomico Banks and the Diamond Shoals off Cape Hatteras.

Although hurricane winds had diminished, huge hurricane-produced waves still rocked the ocean. Without its anchors, the *Deering* could not stop. Navigation was tricky, and the *Deering* was unable to respond to immediate navigation inputs. What if this was a live mine and they were being pushed toward it? Quick action must be taken. Abandon ship!

Knowing that if the schooner were destroyed the retreating crew would need critical navigation tools and charts, these were all quickly gathered. Crew also hastily gathered essential personal belongings, leaving the prepared food behind. Unable to locate the six-toed cat in their panic, it was also left behind as the crew set off in the lifeboats.

Some pieces of this puzzle had already been put in place earlier. When Captain Merritt had become ill, he and his son left the ship in Lewes, Delaware, to seek emergency medical attention. In their haste to pack up, one pair of the captain's boots had been overlooked and left behind in his cabin.

The hostilities between substitute captain Wormell and new first mate McLellan had been brewing from the outset. When they finally erupted on board, a fistfight broke out between the two men on January 23. Wormell was knocked out and suffered a concussion, remaining unconscious. McLellan put Wormell in the captain's cabin and took over command of the ship. His handwriting now appeared on the ship's map. He stayed in the extra bed in the captain's cabin to keep an eye on

Wormell, and had another mate stay there when McLellan was busy running the ship. McLellan also granted his crew much greater freedom, allowing them to roam where previously prohibited.

The condition of the ship and the incompetence of the crew now placed the *Deering* in imminent peril. They hailed the Cape Lookout Lightship to record their condition and position so that help would be on the way. It was what McLellan had been wanting, except for one grievous fact: They were now in extreme danger. In a further request for help, they sent the red lights up the mast. When that did not work, they abandoned ship with the hope that the seas would calm down while they waited nearby, after which they would return to the ship and continue the voyage.

However, the commander here at the infamous Diamond Shoals was the Graveyard of the Atlantic, not McLellan. The doomed plan saw the *Deering* run helplessly hard aground. Their small, fragile lifeboats became death-boats, driven far out to sea and sinking in a watery grave, leaving no trace. Mystery explained.

Our Evidence for This Theory?

Actually, none. We made all of this up. This was just an exercise to construct a scenario in which all the clues fit. All of the proposed theories do not hold water, for one reason or another. This is the first theory to account for all of the actual existing facts, circumstances, and clues. *Semper Paratus!*

Finding Answers

The single best source of information on this wreck, amassing a huge volume of details and evidence through incredible research, is Bland Simpson's 2002 book, *Ghost Ship of Diamond Shoals*. In his 244 pages, Simpson does not espouse a single theory, but rather provides an amazing amount of facts, inviting readers to draw their own conclusions.

CHAPTER 17
M & E HENDERSON

Three foreign crewmen were discovered staggering aimlessly on the Hatteras Island beaches near New Inlet. The ship, and its crew of four, was a total loss. Speaking no English, the survivors could not provide an explanation. These foreigners were arrested and imprisoned because "they probably did it."

The Ship

As is the case with so many stories from the Outer Banks, the facts about this wreck are contradictory and controversial. Such is the nature of a mystery, for by definition, there is no proven answer. The two most reliable sources (David Stick, author of *Graveyard of the Atlantic*, and Joe Mobley, author of *Ship Ashore!*) tell the same story, which follows.

The *M & E Henderson* was a 387-ton, three-masted schooner hailing from Philadelphia. She was already an older ship by late November of 1879 when she departed from the port of Bull River, South Carolina, bound for Baltimore, Maryland, with a heavy cargo of phosphate rock.

The crew of seven consisted of four white men—the captain, two mates, and a cook—and three Spanish mulatto deckhands.

The Mystery Begins

Around sunset on November 29, 1879, the *M & E Henderson* had been seen north of Cape Hatteras sailing north, toward New Inlet. She was observed to be perilously close to shore, although not in actual danger at that time.

Surfman Tillett had been on beach patrol, traveling south from his Pea Island Station, reaching New Inlet by four a.m. It took Tillett another hour or so to return to his station. No shipwrecks—not even a ship—had been spotted. True to their training, after lighting a fire in the stove for the cook, Tillett climbed the stairs to the watchtower. On this clear, calm, moonlit night, looking out of the south window and using his "marine glass," Tillett saw a man on the beach. His sudden appearance was odd, since Tillett had seen no one when completing his patrol in that area. Realizing that the mysterious man on the beach could possibly be a shipwreck victim, Tillett alerted the keeper and crew. Heading south, the lifesavers came upon the man, disheveled and obviously exhausted. He was a foreigner who could not speak coherent English, but soon made it clear that his ship's masts were gone, and the captain had drowned.

They learned later that at five a.m., the same time that Tillett had returned to the station, the schooner *M & E Henderson* had "struck on the bar at the north point of New Inlet, North Carolina, and went to pieces within an hour,"[1] according to that year's USLSS Annual Report.

Suspecting that this might be the case, the lifesavers rushed the survivor back to the station for succor from the cook, who remained at the station. The lifesavers then set out to look for more possible survivors. About a mile and a quarter south, the Annual Report continued, "they came upon a great strew of debris from the wreck, and saw, at the same time, some part of the vessel rising and falling upon the sea in the moonlight, about three hundred yards from shore."[2] Today, this is called flotsam and jetsam. Maritime law defines this as marine debris associated with vessels. Flotsam is debris not deliberately thrown overboard and is often the result of shipwrecks. Jetsam is the debris which is

Surfman on beach patrol dressed in what the LSS regulations state is his "storm suit," made of "rubber or unbleached duck cloth treated with linseed oil" and embossed with the letters LSS. *He wears a regulation "southwester hat" and carries a lit lantern in his right hand, an optional walking stick in his left. Boots were non-regulation and up to each individual surfman. Across his chest is strapped the Costin flares used to simultaneously signal both the shipwreck and his station.*
Courtesy US Coast Guard

deliberately thrown overboard—for example, to lighten the load of a ship in distress—and may be in the water or washed ashore.

Going another three-quarters of a mile, the lifesavers arrived at New Inlet, which marks the end of that island. They came upon fishermen there who said they had found one sailor "floating in the channel." They rescued him, brought him to their camp at Jack's Shoal, revived him, and gave him dry clothes.

The Good Samaritan fisherman, joined by most of the lifesaving crew, continued looking for other survivors around New Inlet. However, the keeper and two surfmen wanted to see the survivor at the fishermen's camp, so they boated over to Jack's Shoal. On the way there, they saw a bewildered man sitting on the beach who appeared "quite insensible." (This would be called "shock" today.) Here, unfortunately, we find

NEW INLET AND INLAND SOUND ISLANDS

New Inlet: This was a break, or inlet, located between Hatteras Island and Pea Island, connecting the Pamlico Sound to the Atlantic Ocean. It was called an inlet because it allowed ships to get into the sound. A better name would be "outlets," for the freshwater from the sound flows out through them to the ocean. New Inlet was first recorded on a map in 1738. It was closed in 1922, but a 1933 hurricane reopened it. It was closed again a few months later by another storm. Hurricane Irene was the latest storm to reopen this inlet in 2011. NCDOT decided to build a temporary bridge, which was replaced by the permanent bridge dedicated in 2018 as the Captain Richard Etheridge Bridge.

Inland Sound Islands: These islands dot the western side just offshore of Hatteras Island. Some are tiny and often not named, but others are large and named. All are uninhabited, and thus make exciting places to hunt, fish, or explore. Examples include, from Oregon Inlet to Rodanthe: Eagle Nest Point, Goat Island, Goose Island, Pea Island Point, Jesse Shoals, St. Clair Lump, Cat Island, and Jack's Shoal.

conflicting details. One reliable source shows that this nearly uncon-scious man was hurried to the fishermen's camp and treated. The other reliable report states that he was taken to the Life-Saving Station for restoration. Either way, his life was saved.

Of the four missing and presumed drowned, only two bodies were recovered. Sadly, this was almost three weeks later, so the bodies, badly decomposed, were respectfully buried on the beach.

A Nearly Unfortunate Ending

The three foreign-born survivors, unable to comprehend or speak English, could offer no accounts of what had actually happened. To some people at the time, the fact that a ship was ruined and all four white men perished, yet all three dark-skinned men survived, was suspicious. The ship's owner swore out a warrant and the Spaniards were arrested, spending months in a Baltimore jail, awaiting trial. Due to a lack of evidence, they were released.

Another Outer Banks Shipwreck Mystery Is Born

The USLSS Annual Report of 1880 summarized the investigation in a single sentence: "The cause of the loss of the vessel remains mysterious."[3]

VI.

DRAMATIC
FAILURES

CHAPTER 18

RMS *TITANIC*

Although this most dramatic of shipwreck stories far from the Outer Banks is well known to the public through movies, documentaries, investigations, research reports, and magazine articles, there is a mysterious Outer Banks connection: An SOS-type message was received at the Hatteras US Weather Bureau—and what happened to that message is shocking.

No shipwreck in history has received more coverage than that of the RMS *Titanic*.

Books written about the disaster numbered 174 by 2018. Seventeen movies have been made, ranging from the 20th Century Fox James Cameron blockbuster of 1997, the newer *Titanic: 20 Years Later with James Cameron* in 2017, to the 1912 short film released only twenty-nine days after the sinking. The latter starred Dorothy Gibson, who was an actual survivor. So far, there have been twenty-nine television and documentary movies, and innumerable newspaper, magazine, and online articles have been written and published. There are 99.6 million Google results when typing in the search term.

We all know the basic story very well. In the spring of 1912, the largest ship ever to sail the seas, the RMS *Titanic*, left Southampton on her maiden voyage. On her way to New York, she struck an iceberg and sank within hours. The death toll was the largest maritime disaster in the history of passenger voyages.

RMS

The disaster led to sensational reports and created numerous studies and investigations. The 2017 James Cameron documentary theorized that the sinking was more directly caused by massive coal fires that lasted for days in the ship's bunkers, starting ten days before sailing, cleverly referenced as "A Story of Fire and Ice."

The story that almost everyone knows is that around midnight on April 14, 1912, the RMS *Titanic* struck an equally enormous iceberg which sliced a huge gash in her starboard hull. The icy Atlantic relentlessly poured in, taking only three hours to send the gargantuan ship to the ocean floor, taking with her to their deaths 1,500 of the 2,200 passengers. This enormous tragedy continues to generate articles, discussions, documentaries, emotions, and even legends.

We are not here to advocate for certain theories or explore mysteries of this disaster. It seems unlikely that anything could be added to this massively covered saga; plus, this was hundreds of miles from anywhere on the North Carolina coast. So why is it in this book?

There is, in fact, a largely unknown yet extremely significant Outer Banks connection to the *Titanic* tragedy—so significant, in fact, that it might have prevented the enormous loss of life.

The Unsinkable Ship

As with so many other chapters in this book, the facts about the sinking of the *Titanic* are contradictory. It is important for our story to understand that, right or wrong, the public perception in 1912 was that this new ship was unsinkable. In 1912, the RMS *Titanic* was the largest man-made object in the world. Before the *Titanic* sailed in 1912, Philip Franklin, White Star Line vice president, blatantly stated that the ship was "unsinkable."[1] Passenger Margaret Devaney said, "I took passage on the *Titanic* for I thought it would be a safe steamship and I had heard it could not sink." Then there was the legendary and often-repeated crewman's reassurance to a nervous passenger: "God himself could not sink this ship!" It is used in the Cameron film. Whatever its origin, there is no doubt that people did believe *Titanic* to be unsinkable, which helps to explain what happened next on the Outer Banks.

The Outer Banks Connection

Being a center of weather-making, its surrounding waters already known as "The Graveyard of the Atlantic," the US Weather Bureau had set up a number of weather stations in various coastal towns, villages, lighthouses, and life-saving stations from 1871 to 1904.

In July of 1901, Secretary James Wilson of the US Department of Agriculture awarded a contract to C. L. Harding to design and build a weather station in Hatteras Village, the southernmost of Hatteras

US WEATHER BUREAU— THE EVOLUTION

Instituted by President Ulysses S. Grant in 1870, the main purpose of the US Weather Bureau (USWB) was to give weather data to military posts and US Navy ships. It was placed under the jurisdiction of the Secretary of War (now Defense) and operated by the US Army Signal Service. The USWB became civilian in 1890, with a focus on aiding farmers, and was run under the Department of Agriculture. In 1940 the Bureau was transferred to the Department of Commerce. Finally, in 1966, the agency became part of the National Oceanic and Atmospheric Administration (NOAA), and was renamed today's National Weather Service.

Actual shot of the 1902 Hatteras Weather Bureau Station, with lots of detail.
Courtesy National Park Service, Cape Hatteras National Seashore

Island's seven villages. The two-story cellar frame and brick building was officially commissioned and became operational on January 1, 1902.

Working late into the night of Sunday, April 14, 1912, station operators Richard Dailey and Horace Gaskins received an urgent telegram message at 11:25 p.m.

The telegraph message received by the Hatteras Weather Bureau Station contained the words "CQD: Have Struck Iceberg." It was from the RMS *Titanic*. Dailey and Gaskins immediately forwarded the message to USWB headquarters, located at New York Station. It was received by twenty-one-year-old David Sarnoff (future president of RCA). Like everyone else at the time, Sarnoff "knew" that the *Titanic* was unsinkable, so he severely chastised the Hatteras senders. In his response, he said that the senders were troublemakers just "clogging up the lines," and that they were to refrain from any further communications.

This would directly relate to 1,514 deaths. (Four different sources report the number as 1,496, 1,503, 1,517, and this one, 1,514. The 2017 *National Geographic* special, Titanic: *20 Years Later with James Cameron*,

TELEGRAPH, TELEGRAM, AND C.Q.D.

The telegraph was invented and developed by Samuel Morse during the 1830s and first transmitted successfully in 1844, so this was already established technology by the time of the *Titanic*. It was the fastest communication at the time, traveling with the speed of electricity. It worked by sending electric signals over wires. Letters were created using a series of short or long beeps, called dots and dashes. The receiving operators would write down the letters, forming a message. This paper record became the telegram.

C.Q.D. (also CQD) and later SOS were distress signals first sent by telegraph. Both are the subject of very popular misconceptions. The term "CQ" was the English hearing of the French word *secu*, pronounced "see-cue," meaning "security." This was to precede a secure, important message; it was an alert, saying, "Stations, listen up!" The D was added by Marconi stations in 1904 to indicate "distress." As always, when things don't make sense, we make up stories to help them make sense. Unfortunately, CQD never meant "Come Quickly, Distress." The internationally recognized signal for distress was replaced not long after with "SOS." This was chosen simply because the letter for S is three dots and O is three dashes, so they could be typed quickly and easily. Sorry; this never meant "Save Our Ship."

puts it emphatically at 1,496. Many other sources simply say "over 1,500.")

Here, another *Titanic* mystery is born. Investigations of Sarnoff's logbook showed that he signed off at ten p.m. that night, almost two hours before that stern reply. So, who sent it, or why? We do not know.

Tragically, the error was compounded.

The steamship RMS *Carpathia* was the nearest ship to *Titanic*'s reported position, being only sixty-seven miles away. They had also received distress messages from the *Titanic*. In Hatteras Village,

Re–creation of the Titanic's *"Marconi Room," with the telegraph.*
Public Domain

THE MOST POPULAR
TITANIC LEGEND

The story of the Unsinkable Molly Brown is an audience favorite. There was a real Margaret Brown whose nickname was Maggie. A wealthy American socialite and philanthropist, she was a first-class passenger on the *Titanic*'s maiden voyage and a survivor, in Lifeboat No. 6. The legend revolves around Mrs. Brown's unusual reactions to the disaster. Apparently true are the facts that she helped others into the lifeboat before boarding herself, and that she even took an oar herself. What is undocumented is the legend that she urged the crewman in charge to return to the debris field to look for more survivors. Even so, it made too good a story to pass up, inspiring the 1960 Broadway musical and the 1964 MGM movie of the same title, starring Debbie Reynolds. There is a more recent and interesting documentary, Titanic: *20 Years Later with James Cameron* (2017), featuring Maggie's granddaughter, Muffet Laurie Brown.

weather bureau operators Dailey and Gaskins also received this tele-graph traffic. Due to their previous reprimand, they did not forward this second message to the New York office.

Fortunately, the *Carpathia* did eventually respond, but almost too late. Nevertheless, she managed to save 701 survivors.

History Nearly Lost

The telegram incident lay fallow for almost one hundred years. The 1901 Hatteras Weather Bureau Station was decommissioned in 1946 and then used for Weather Bureau and Park Service personnel living quarters. It was turned over to the US Coast Guard and occupied from 1952 to 1958, then transferred to the National Park Service (NPS). From 1958 to 1976 the building became a research center used by Duke University and North Carolina State University. From 1995 to 2001 it remained vacant, which is never a good thing for an old building. Fortunately, restoration work was started in 2001 and finished in 2005, resulting in a gorgeous building, both inside and out. In the summer of 2007, it became an official Outer Banks Visitor Bureau Welcome Center downstairs and a Weather Bureau museum upstairs, and remains open to the public today.

In the course of the restoration in 2005, workers were removing old newspapers and crumpled documents from the walls which had been used as insulation. Some of the original pages that had been ripped from the station logbook were discovered. They were sent to NPS Headquarters in Harpers Ferry for restoration and then returned to the NPS in Manteo, where they remained unseen for another eigh-teen months. Cape Hatteras Seashore Park historian (retired) Douglas Stover later began to go over these papers. He strained to make out the barely legible writing, eventually discerning the words *Titanic* CQD. It proved to be a monumental discovery. Although it made national headlines at the time, this aspect of the *Titanic* tragedy remains largely unknown to the general public today.

The original document was briefly displayed at the North Carolina Museum of Natural Sciences. It found its permanent home in the most appropriate place—the Graveyard of the Atlantic Museum (chapter 2) in nearby Hatteras Village, only a few miles from the Weather Bureau. The original logbook page is on display. The text reads:

> Received Hatteras Station at 11:25 p.m. TITANIC calling C.Q.D. giving reading 41.44 about 380 miles SSE of Cape Race. At 11:35 p.m. TITANIC gives corrected position as 41.46 N 50.14W. A matter of five or six miles difference. He says "have struck iceberg."

The Significance

Joe Schwarzer, director of the three North Carolina maritime museums, which includes the Graveyard of the Atlantic Museum, says, "The significance of the telegram is it is physical evidence of the very moment when the ship was not going to be saved."[2] This is a chilling thought to the visitor who stands in front of the actual document, knowing what came next.

Albert Ervin, the special exhibits coordinator for the Graveyard of the Atlantic Museum, says about this notice, "It is one of the earliest, if not the earliest, because of the time we typically hear that the *Titanic* hit the iceberg is 11:40 p.m." Yet the Hatteras Weather Bureau log reports receiving the message at 11:25 p.m. *Titanic's* first distress message was recorded as 12:15 a.m., her time. A corrected message was sent at 12:25 a.m. (That would be 11:25 p.m., Hatteras time—an exact match.) Ervin concludes, "I think people are really surprised and fascinated that there is a North Carolina connection." Also enormously significant was the public's belief in 1912 that any ship could be unsinkable. Joe Schwarzer adds, "There was blind faith in technology, a belief that a powerful ship couldn't sink."[3]

Had that not been the popular mind-set at the time, then everyone would have realized that any ship faced the possibility of sinking. Everyone also knew at the time that striking an iceberg was a notorious

TITANIC DOMINOES

- Creating *the* largest man-made object on Earth produced public awe;
- The conception that the super-luxury gargantuan ship was unsinkable;
- A coal workers' strike was on at the time;
- Coal bunker fires were not uncommon, and the danger was overlooked;
- Tight schedule and expected press coverage pressured decision to launch without extinguishing coal fires;
- Spreading of fire to other bunkers required putting burning coals into adjacent boilers, thereby increasing speed;
- Iceberg warnings were ignored;
- Watertight bulkheads did not go all the way up to the next deck;
- CQD from Hatteras was dismissed;
- Not enough lifeboats on board;
- Lifeboats not filled to capacity;
- Random firing of flares did not create distress signal, delaying nearby response of *Carpathia*.

cause of a ship sinking, and that "CQD" was an urgent distress call. If these facts could have been grasped then, under vastly different circumstances, it is extremely likely that the rescue would have been significantly faster and more successful.

A foolish belief in the impossible led to fatally flawed decisions, creating a deadly chain of dominoes that resulted in the most dramatic maritime failure of all time.

CHAPTER 19

USS *HURON*

A movie scriptwriter would be hard-pressed to create a fictitious story with more disastrous circumstances, bad luck, and a chain reaction of calamity than the true story of the Navy ship USS Huron.

The Ship

The USS *Huron* was a federal gunboat, often referred to as a man-of-war steamer. She was built in Chester, Pennsylvania, commissioned in 1875, and named for the Great Lake, over five hundred miles away. The *Huron* was one of the last "in between old and modern" ships—she, the *Alert*, and the *Ranger* were the last to be built of iron instead of steel. Plus, she was a combination of steam-powered engines and full-rigged sails, just in case.

The Saga Begins

The USS *Huron* was only two years old when this sad saga began. *Huron*'s commander, George Ryan, had left New York bound for the Caribbean for a military surveying expedition. On the way *Huron* put in at Norfolk, Virginia (commonly called the Hampton Roads area), for coal and supplies, and was set to depart immediately. Instead, orders

The USS Huron *in better days. She was built in the transition period from sails to steam, and had both.*
Courtesy Naval Historical Center

came to wait for a government draftsman to come on board. This took an additional annoying three days.

On the fourth day, Friday, November 23, 1877, defying maritime conventions, the *Huron* departed Hampton Roads. For centuries, Christian sailors had *never* left port on a Friday (the day Christ was crucified). Additionally, storm flags had been flying since Wednesday. What was the *Huron* doing? What was Ryan thinking? Bad omens from the start. Noteworthy is the fact that on this day, not only were *no other* ships seen departing, in fact, the only two ships that the *Huron* saw at all were coming in for the safety of port.

Heading for Disaster

The distance between Norfolk, Virginia, and Nags Head, North Carolina, is only sixty-two nautical miles, normally an easy, short trip. For

AMAZING PREMONITION

Lt. Arthur H. Fletcher was the previous executive officer of the *Huron* and was on board when it docked at Hampton Roads. He had been plagued by a vision of the awful demise of his ship.

After his repeated requests for a transfer had been denied, he simply jumped ship and deserted right then and there, before the *Huron* sailed.

Commander Ryan and his entire crew, however, it would be neither. In fact, it would be the opposite in every sense. It was fraught with problems right from the start. Winds were already at seventy miles per hour, nearly hurricane force. Ryan would have to fight the Gulf Stream current, moving steadily and powerfully in the opposite direction the *Huron* was going. To do that, Ryan had the same two choices ships' captains have had for centuries: go far out to sea to the east to avoid the current, or hug the coast and stay inside of it. The first was safer but took longer. The second was much quicker but much more dangerous. Still, Commander Ryan had faith in his new, iron-hulled ship, surely stronger than this gale.

These sea captain choices and circumstances sound ominously familiar. The captain of the famous tourist ship, the HMS *Bounty*, made the same choices for the same reasons in the same area during Hurricane Sandy in October—nearly the same month—of 2012. Tragically the results were the same for that ship, but turned out triumphantly for the crew, save two. Our modern Coast Guard rescued fourteen of the sixteen crew in the middle of that hurricane (see chapter 7 for the full story).

The Final Straw

A small navigational miscalculation after the *Huron* passed the Currituck Beach Lighthouse but before reaching the Bodie Island Lighthouse indicated the *Huron* to be farther offshore than she actually was.

The USS *Huron*

The terrible final moments of the USS Huron *on that early morning of November 24, 1877, are captured dramatically in this period engraving.*
East Carolina University

At 1:30 in the morning on a bitterly cold and blustery November 24, the *Huron* ran hard aground. It was so violent that she badly stuck. Incredibly, she was only two hundred yards offshore of the Nags Head beach.

The foremast and mainmast were gone, and already several sailors had been swept from the decks into oblivion. In spite of the potential disaster, the crew responded in a disciplined, military manner. They began trying to right the ship and free her from the bar. They had all learned the lessons of shipwrecks from earlier times: Stay on the ship!

Against All Odds—and the Odds Won

The constant high winds, the relentless pounding surf, and the bitter cold that kept getting worse would soon combine to take their deadly toll. By two a.m., just thirty minutes after she had grounded, the steam engines died. No power remained to help her get unstuck. Gradually the stern started sinking and the hull began to roll onto its port side. Orders were given for all hands to go forward.

Were it that Hollywood movie, appropriately, Chris Pine from *The Finest Hours* would star, portraying the real-life hero, Ensign Lucian Young. This handsome twenty-five-year-old had been trained the navy way at Annapolis and had already earned a medal for bravery in the rescue of a fellow sailor in the Mediterranean Sea. Here is the beginning of his ordeal on the *Huron*, in his own words:

> *I had hold of the Gatlin gun, when a heavy sea came over and washed myself and about five others down to leeward. All but myself went under the sail, and they were drowned. I was caught in the bag of the sail and hurt both legs against the gaff, but worked myself forward and succeeded in getting on the top gallant forecastle.*[1]

Then, on his own initiative, Young went below to retrieve signal flares and rockets, came back on deck, and proceeded to shoot them all as a sign of distress. There was no response.

Around dawn, dim figures could be made out on the beach. That was the first time the sailors realized how close they were to salvation! These folks, however, were only locals helplessly watching, as is human nature, to observe tragedy. Close maybe, but a violently drowning sea between them and the shore.

Conditions were worsening by the minute. Literally every new huge wave carried someone off the *Huron* to disappear into the raging surf. By now most of the sailors were gone, and so were all the lifeboats. There was one last resort, and Ensign Young not only seized it, he took firm charge of it.

Remaining on board was a never-used rubber raft called a balsa. It had been stowed so securely that it took Young fifteen minutes to free it. His hands were so numb that he could not open it, so seaman Antonio Williams helped him. Together they launched the raft into the boiling cauldron of the sea below them, with Young and Williams on board. Almost immediately it capsized and trapped them both underwater for so long that they were mere seconds from drowning. Somehow, they got back on, only to have the raft capsize again. And again. And again.

Miraculously, they reached shore—alive, but with injuries. Right next to them were two other sailors, also alive, but so exhausted that they could not get out of the surf. Young dragged them farther up the beach, then directed the locals to start helping any remaining survivors. He asked one to telegraph an emergency message to Washington. Somehow, it got to the Kitty Hawk Station.

In his book *Ship Ashore!*, Joe Mobley writes, "The ultimate and tragic irony was that the Nags Head [USLSS] Station No. 7 stood only two and one-half miles south of the disaster. But in keeping with the Life-Saving Service's then current operating procedure, it remained closed and locked until next month, when the active season began."[2]

Realizing this, after all he had been through, Ensign Young was not about to let a mere lock or permission stand in his way. He gathered several locals, went the two and a half miles to the station, broke in, and gathered the Lyle gun and its accompanying equipment. As if on cue, Sheriff Brinkley from Dare County arrived on a horse-drawn cart that carried all the rescue equipment, accompanying Young to the wreck. By the time they arrived, there was no one left to rescue. Not a soul was left on the *Huron*, dead or alive. The second great irony is that had this very rescue equipment been there with the LSS crew at 1:30 a.m., when the *Huron* had grounded, probably all would have been saved.

It Seemed to Never End

Four ships arrived on scene early the next day, in response to the telegraphed SOS. The sea was still so rough that when a party launched a ship's boat to investigate the wreck, it was capsized and five more were drowned. Of the *Huron*'s crew of 132, only 34 survived. Now the total death toll reached 103.

Bodies washed ashore for the next two weeks, some as far as thirty miles away. There was a huge public outcry nationwide.

Almost before all of the victims could be laid to rest, only two months later and just a few miles north of this tragedy, the *Metropolis*

"I suppose I must spend a little on Lifesaving."

Thomas Nast's political cartoon critical of the federal government following the widely publicized wreck of the Huron. *The caption reads: "US: 'I suppose I must spend a little on Lifesaving service, life-boat stations, life-boats, surf-boats, etc.; but it is too bad to be obliged to waste so much money.'"*
1877 Harpers Weekly, *Courtesy Library of Congress*

wrecked, with a loss of eighty-five lives.[3] The two stories would forever be connected.

Ensign Young was awarded the LSS Gold Medal. The *Huron's* remains still lie 250 yards off a Nags Head beach off Bladen Street, designated with a marker.

The US Life-Saving Service greatly expanded its operations and went on to save over 177,000 lives from the more than 178,000 to which it responded over the course of the rest of its history. It was restructured in June of 1878 well after the wreck of the *Huron* (November 1877) and the *Metropolis* (January 1878)

CHAPTER 20
METROPOLIS

Almost immediately following the disaster of the Huron, *only two months later just twenty miles from that site, the wreck of the* Metropolis *and drowning of hundreds of victims was witnessed by locals and vacationers on the Nags Head beaches. The public outrage generated by Thomas Nast's recent political cartoon so closely coupled with a similar disaster would lead to a total restructuring of the USLSS.*

Still stinging from the humiliating loss of the *Huron* in late 1877, the US Life-Saving Service's reputation was in serious jeopardy. Tragically,

Wreck of the steamship Metropolis *(lithograph,* Harper's Weekly, *December 31, 1877).*
Courtesy Library of Congress

it not only got worse, but did so quickly. Only two months after the *Huron* disaster, and only twenty miles away, the steamer *Metropolis* wrecked, with another eighty-five lives lost.

The infamous wreck of the *Metropolis*, forever tied with the name of the *Huron*, turned out to be the single most important shipwreck in the history of the US Life-Saving Service. Although there is plenty of conflicting information, one thing is clear: Prior to 1878, the USLSS had been ripe with cronyism, nepotism, and "good ol' boy" shenanigans. Posts and positions were granted politically, or as favors, usually to unqualified persons. In addition, there weren't enough stations; they were often unmanned; supplies were illegally used for personal consumption; and training was slack, or even ignored. Consequently, "rescues" were far too often shameful failures. The *Metropolis* was the proverbial straw that broke the camel's back.

Headlines of the *Metropolis* disaster exploded in newspapers all over America. The articles were filled with anger, and the news outraged the entire nation. Demands for immediate improvements had the politicians retreating. Thomas Nast's political cartoon certainly captured the critical essence of the situation.

The Phoenix Arises

It was time for a new and improved US Life-Saving Service. Ironically, it would become *the most* heroic organization in American history. Much of that was due to one man.

Until the Civil War, the United States had only one national maritime organization: the Revenue Marine. It had been fathered by Alexander Hamilton, becoming official in 1790. In 1863 the name was changed to the United States Revenue Cutter Service (USRCS), with a singular mission of ocean-based law enforcement. It was neither charged with nor equipped or trained for lifesaving rescues. Finally recognized in 1871, a US Life-Saving Service (USLSS) was established only as a branch of the USRCS, headed by Sumner Kimball from 1871 until 1878.

As a result of the uproar caused by the *Huron* and *Metropolis* disasters, in 1878 the USLSS was made a separate and equal organization to the US Revenue Cutter Service, and both remained under the Treasury Department. The new service with a new mission needed a dynamic, powerful, and competent "straitlaced" administrator. Kimball was asked to be that superintendent.

Well aware of its poor reputation, Kimball was extremely guarded in his response. In essence, he said he would take over if—and only if—he could do it his way, with official backing, and yet no interference. Having considered the secretary's proposal carefully for a week, Kimball accepted the promotion on the following terms.

> Mr. Secretary, I shall accept your offer upon one condition. If you will stand by me, after I have convinced you that I am right, I shall attempt to bring about the reforms you desire. But I want to warn you that the pressure will be tremendous. Congressmen will come to you in long processions and will attempt to convince you that I am wrong and that the service is being ruined. It will require an uncommon display of backbone on your part, but if you will stand firm and refer all complaints to me, I promise you that I shall put the service where you want it and where it ought to be.[1]

So it would be.

Born in Maine on September 2, 1834, and raised there, Sumner Increase Kimball became a lawyer in 1858. He was elected to the Maine House of Representatives the following year, became a clerk in the US Treasury Department in 1862, and became superintendent of the USRCS in 1871. He had always had a stellar reputation for honesty, competence, and accomplishments. He personally remained out of the spotlight and simply focused on organization efficiency. He remained as superintendent of the USLSS for thirty-seven years, until 1915, when it became the US Coast Guard.

Scholar Dr. Dennis Noble writes:

Kimball was unquestionably the driving force behind the United States' possessing a first-class lifesaving organization. Much of the present-day Coast Guard's highly regarded reputation as a humanitarian organization is the result of his organizational skills and management abilities. Many of the routines that he established, such as constant drills with rescue equipment, are just as important today as they were more than a century ago. In the final analysis Kimball was the ultimate bureaucrat: he knew how to work within the federal government . . . Kimball realized that to create a professional service, and one that was in large part located in small communities, his crews would have to be above petty politics and be seen as a service to the community and the nation.[2]

That is precisely what today's US Coast Guard is! And that is why the *Metropolis* was "the single most important shipwreck in American history." It ushered in Sumner I. Kimball and started his model of efficiency, competence, standardization, and honor, still at the heart of the US Coast Guard today.

The Genesis of the Story

A series of waterfalls on the Mamoré River in Bolivia rendered navigation impossible for the next 180 miles. This blocked additional sailing to the mighty Amazon and then to the Atlantic. In 1877, the Bolivian government contracted P. & T. Collins from Philadelphia to build a 180-mile railroad around the blockade, thereby adding an additional three thousand miles which steamships could ply—an enormous benefit to the economy of Bolivia.

On January 2, 1878, the Collins Company dispatched the first of three ships to Bolivia by way of Brazil. This was the *Mercedita*, with two hundred men, machinery, engines, and five hundred tons of rails from the Philadelphia and Reading Coal and Iron Company. The second and third ships were the *Stars and Stripes* and the *Richmond*.

The Ship

Whether the Collins Company was aware of the suspicious background of the *Stars and Stripes* was unclear, but probably not. She was a former federal gunship in the American Civil War. An older ship, the *Stars and Stripes* was an 879-ton, bark-rigged screw steamer measuring 198 feet from bow to stern with a beam 34 feet wide. She was built in 1861 at the beginning of the war. After the war she was cut in two and lengthened by 40 feet. By the time Collins had acquired the ship, its papers had been altered to show it was built in 1871, making her appear to be ten years younger. There was one other alteration—the *Stars and Stripes* name was changed to the *Metropolis*. Collins was likely unaware that a month earlier the ship had to be towed to harbor because she was disabled. This is the ship he would be taking to distant Brazil with an enormous, heavy load of people and cargo.

The Voyage Begins

Under these false pretenses, the *Metropolis* departed the Reading Railroad wharf in Philadelphia on January 29, 1878. Of the 248 people on board, 215 were railroad workers, 20 were passengers, and she had a crew of 13. Her cargo was 500 tons of iron rails from the same Philadelphia company, 200 tons of supplies, and 250 tons of coal to burn for her two steam engines.

The day the *Metropolis* set sail was a Tuesday. The seas were calm, and the breeze light. As happens so often around the Outer Banks, the weather changed quickly and violently. By the next day, Wednesday, the seas had become choppy at first, and then rough. By that afternoon, the waves were so turbulent that most people were seasick.

Conditions went from bad to worse. A leak from the rudder post was discovered that had put waist-deep water in the bilge. Captain J. H. Ankers (reported as "Aukers" in a 1957 magazine article) was near the Chesapeake Bay at this time, and could have found safe harbor in

HAMPTON ROADS

Hampton Roads can be a confusing designation, for it is not a road, not a place, but rather a geographical area. It refers to the metropolitan area surrounding the major Virginia cities of Norfolk, Hampton, Chesapeake, Virginia Beach, Portsmouth, Suffolk, Newport News, and some of northeastern North Carolina. It also can refer to the body of water surrounding that area.

nearby Hampton Roads. Instead, he decided to continue and to lighten the ship by jettisoning an estimated 50 tons of her coal cargo.

However, more serious trouble was brewing. The constant pounding of the waves on the leaky old ship started to shift the improperly loaded five hundred tons of steel rails. As this continued, the shifting rails began to open the vessel's seams. "Then, without warning, a huge wave broke completely over the vessel, taking away the smoke stack, seven of the lifeboats, the steam whistle, the engine-room ventilators, sky light, after-mainsail, starboard saloon, and most of the gangway,"[3] as described by David Stick in his classic book, *Graveyard of the Atlantic.*

The Tragedy

Just before dawn on Thursday, the ship was completely helpless, so Captain Ankers decided to beach her. She struck Currituck Beach at 6:00 a.m. Notice here that the *New York Times* article of January 31, 1878, said the time was *6:30 p.m.*, just another example of conflicting and erroneous "facts" that caused confusion. The wreck was on the bar about three miles south of the Currituck Beach Lighthouse and four miles south from the Life-Saving Station there. However, this was ten miles north of the Kitty Hawk Life-Saving Station, which was the only station in the area connected to the outside world by telegraph. That promised to be of vital importance in getting help, but the message delivered by a boy on scene who left too soon turned out to be inaccurate. More factual confusion.

Keeper John G. Chappel of LSS Station No. 4, Currituck Beach, set off at 11:30 a.m., five hours after the wreck, late and ill-prepared. Stick continues:

> While the Keeper was thus engaged the six remaining lifesav-
> ers from Station Number Four were laboriously dragging their
> heavily laden cart toward the scene. . . . It is doubtful that it was
> within the capabilities of the six human beings to haul that cart
> the full distance to the wreck. All of them had been on beach
> patrol during the night and had walked from twelve to thirty-
> two miles along the flooded beach on the lookout for stranded
> vessels.[4]

In a 1951 article of *The State*, editor Bill Sharpe accurately points out:

> It also must be remembered that the delay in the rescuers
> reaching the wreck, which the terrified passengers mistook for
> indifference, the magnitude of the calamity and the hysteria
> incident to such a disaster led to many wild and unfounded or
> exaggerated reports, many of which were printed and faithfully
> believed.[5]

When the lifesavers reached the wreck about noon, the tragedy would be compounded. In their rush, they had not checked supplies and assumed that all was well. The lifesavers had unknowingly left the station with only enough powder for two shots and not enough projectiles, or "shots." Fortunately, a local resident had a supply of dry powder nearby. This was used for all four unsuccessful shots, and then they were out of projectiles to fire from the Lyle gun. Dr. D. G. Green, the vessel's surgeon, said:

> The scene was beyond description, the eye alone can tell it
> truthfully. There were not enough life-buoys, and many poor
> souls were vainly seeking for them. . . . Dozens were in the water,

THE METROPOLIS.

Unseaworthy Condition of the Wrecked Steamer.

Burying the Dead and Selling the Material Saved from the Wreck—Relief for the Families of the Men who were Drowned.

WASHINGTON, D. C., February 2. The Signal Service Station at the wreck of the Metropolis, reports at 8:30 A. M. to the Chief Signal Office, as follows: "The survivors will leave here at 12 M., to-day, by the steamer Cygnet, for Norfolk. They are destitute of clothing, and most all are barefooted and barcheaded. They are being well cared for by the people."

THE VESSEL BREAKING UP.

NORFOLK, Va., February 2. The wrecking tugs have all returned from the scene of the wreck of the Metropolis, and report that a terrible surf is breaking all along the shore, with a strong southerly current. Very little of the wreck is visible, and it is the opinion of wreckers that the steamer grounded at low tide, with her side exposed to the sweep of the surf, thereby causing much loss of life, the people on her decks being unable to hold on.

AN AUCTION SALE ON THE BEACH.

WASHINGTON, D. C., February 2. The station at the wreck of the Metropolis reports at 1 P. M. to the Chief Signal officer as follows: "The material strewn along the beach, from the wrecked steamer, is now being sold at public auction."

A ROTTEN STERN POST.

NORFOLK, Va., February 2. Michael Glennan, proprietor of the Virginian, has just arrived from the scene of the wreck of the Metropolis, and reports the most doeful state of affairs. The engineer had to wade in water waist deep trying to find the leak, which appeared to be in the stern. The indications are that the leak was caused by the heel of the stern post being perfectly rotten. Captain Glennan thinks the life stations were sinned against than sinning. The stations are ten miles apart, and seven men are expected to patrol the intervening beach. The survivors of the wreck will arrive to-morrow morning, and leave on Monday for Philadelphia.

RELICS FROM THE WRECK

The Signal Service Observer at Cape Hatteras, reports at 3:45 P. M. to the Chief Signal Officer as follows: A yawl boat, some clothing and a pocketbook were washed ashore about a mile from this station to-day. The pocketbook contained the charges of a man by the name of James A. Bowen. I cannot get a clue from what vessel these articles came.

BODIES RECOVERED AND BURIED.

The station at the wreck of the Metropolis reports to the Chief Signal Officer at 4:45 P. M. as follows: Captain Aukers left at 3 P. M. for Norfolk. After the auction of the wrecked material the scene of the wreck was deserted. The keeper of No. 1 station buried fifteen bodies washed up during the night from one mile to eight miles north of his station. One man had a gold plated watch and gold chain; also five keys, which are in the keeper's possession. About 120 of the rescued will go to Norfolk on the steamer Cygnet to-day and will probably reach there by midnight. They are in a very destitute condition and in great need of clothing. Blankets were furnished by the men of the cutter from the steamer Plymouth.

THE METROPOLIS RELIEF FUND.

PHILADELPHIA, February 2. An impromptu meeting of merchants and business men was held to-day, at the Commercial Exchange, to take action in regard to relief for the families of the men who went down on the Metropolis. F. M. Brooke was chosen President, and B. K. Jamison Treasurer. It was resolved to open subscription lists at the office of the Treasurer, to give an opportunity to the citizens to contribute to so worthy an object.

NORFOLK, Va., February 2. Only sixty-eight bodies have been recovered from the wreck of the Metropolis, and through the influence and friendship of Mr. Poynor, of the Currituck Club, they have been buried for identification.

The correspondent of the Associated Press having been delayed by the grounding of the boat, reached the scene of the Metropolis disaster Saturday morning, where he found that the bodies of the dead, so far as recovered, had been buried, and the survivors, having been hospitably cared for, were assembling at Van Slack's Landing from the various points on Currituck Beach, at which they had found shelter.

At the scene of the wreck the beach was strewn with the debris of the ship and cargo from a distance of fifty yards to one mile north of the wreck. The ship was evidently completely broken up, her starboard bilge from fore to main chains having drifted on shore somewhat compact, and containing several, perhaps a dozen or twenty, of the rails which, formed a part of her cargo.

Of the wreck itself, stationary on the spot on which the ship grounded, the boilers and a portion of the engine alone were visible above the breakers, while washing to and fro in the surf, but evidently confined to the bottom in some way, was a portion of the port bow, and astern the ragged ends of the stern and quarter frames as each succeeding surge of the subsiding surf swept on. No doubts are entertained of the recovery of all the iron stowed in the lower hold, as the ship drove well on the beach, and the wreck now lies in about six feet at mean low water.

THE SURVIVORS.

The steamer Cygnet took up the following survivors at Van Stacks and Church's Island and brought them to Norfolk to-night: Wm. Harrison, Richard Clark, James Trimper, Edward Burns, James Goodoyne Christ. Hoehr, Edward McFadden, John McCue, Patrick Rainey, Michael Kline, Arthur McCullough, John Dorrity, Hugh Reily, William Clinton, Michael Casey, Patrick Dillon, William Spellman, John Kelly, John Dorsey, Curtis Cowles, James Moclare, Barney Marshall, Archer McKenley, Patrick Fay, Michael Kelly, John McCabe, John Klink, Daniel McClellan, John Kennedy, John McDevitt, Nicholas Hawkins, Abbott Farnham, John Henry, Thos. Battles, Michael Ryan, J. Carson, C. Benson, W. Sweeney, J. Morrison John Monaghan, Peter Jackson, Charles Marley, James Leslie, Neal O'Donnell, Peter Murphy, James Burns, A. C. Caton, Ceas. Gilbert, Robert Buchan, John Dillon, James Kirruey, Michael Buron, John McNamara, Lawrence McQuitlan, David Welsh, Edward Welsh, Felix Johnson, John McGuire, Pat. McIlvaine, Michael Kenny, Joseph Campbell, Francis Fitzpatrick, Wm. McGinley, Alex. Dougherty, Pat. Welsh, Wm. Gallagher, John McGillan, Jerry Eagan, Mughey Boyle, John McGarry, Pat. Quinn, David Anderson, James Clark, John Murphy, Thos. Farnham, Thomas McDermott, James Cain, John McPeck, George Gundlach, James Maloney, William J. Loftus, Michael McNamee, Wm. Kerwick, Timothy O'Brien, Edward Scully, Wm. Shoeney, Michael Dolan, David Lee, Wm. McLaughlin, Dan'l O'Brien, Jas. Carson, Jno. Bradley, Patrick Gormon, T. Harrington, Jno. Turley, Hugh Brennan, Henry L. Brooke, J. A. Cooney, John McKenna, Richard Dalton, Flavion Huot, Ann Huot, Wm. Hazy, James Dougherty, John Bunker, Frank G. Wynn, Garrett Doyle, John Sherman, John Barry, Thomas Jayne, John Welch, Frank Elliott, James McGuire, Charles Zahner, Thomas Phillips, Michael Welch, James Polan, William King, James Manning, Patrick Curran, Patrick Murphy, Daniel Sweeney.

Detailed newspaper account of the wreck of the Metropolis, *from the* Brooklyn Daily Eagle, *February 3, 1878.*
Public Domain

struggling for their lives, and I saw many a good swimmer killed. . . . I am unable to relate how I saved myself, as I was insensible.[6]

Then a remarkable thing happened, something that would become typical of future lifesavers. "For a mile or more along that wreck-strewn beach, brave men, singly and in groups, waded into the deadly surf at risk of their own lives to rescue people they had never seen before."[7] The new, true lifesavers would not know fatigue or fear or retreat—just their job: saving lives in peril from the sea.

Huron and *Metropolis*, two ships. Two months apart. Twenty miles apart. Not enough Life-Saving Stations. The ones there, without sufficient funding or training. Another loss of 188 total persons. Accusations and counteraccusations.

Near his conclusion, Sharpe says, "In all the hundreds of thousands of words written about the *Metropolis*, then and since, no single person involved in the tragedy escaped ugly charges or bemoaning insinuations."

THE CATASTROPHE THAT SHOOK AMERICA AND LED TO ESTABLISHMENT OF ALL-YEAR BEACH CONTROL BY OUR COAST GUARD

Nothing good could come out of such a ghastly, pitiful wreck as that of the *Metropolis*, it seemed. The steamship came ashore in a heavy sea below Whaleshead (Currituck) Light January 31, 1878, and 103 lives were lost.

Everything about the tragedy was shameful. The owners were charged with concealing defects in the ship, inspectors charged with collusion, the chartering company was accused of overloading her and the captain was accused of imprudent handling of his ship. The Life-Saving crew reached the wreck late, and then without sufficient equipment.

Worst of all, natives of the Bank as well as passengers were accused of inhospitality and looting. Coming on the heels of the scandalous wreck of the warship *Huron* in 1877 off Kitty Hawk, the disaster threw the county into an uproar. The *New York Tribune* carried columns of the story on its front pages, and even months later reverberations . . . in the form of charges, counter-charges, investigation and reports . . . were being heard.

But no matter. As long as men trod that lonely, violent beach, they will always remember the *Metropolis* as one of the too-often times when man's mistakes and inadequacies and greed coincided with a cruel mood of nature to shock the nation with a brutal episode of the sea.[8] Great good did come out of this tragedy after all: Sumner Kimball.

CHAPTER 21

SS *CENTRAL AMERICA*

The true story of gold, greed, and gales has all the dramatic elements of high-seas fiction—but it was real. It took place off the North Carolina coast and resulted in one of the largest and most valuable shipwreck salvages of all time. It also drastically changed American history.

The story of the SS *Central America* has much in common with other chapters in this book—the HMS *Bounty*, the *Queen Anne's Revenge*, the *Tiger* and the Lost Colony, the *Carroll A. Deering*, the *Huron* and *Metropolis*, and, most of all, the RMS *Titanic*. All are subjects of innumerable articles, books, documentaries, and films, and many of the stories contain conflicting information. They all share the element of extreme human real-life drama.

The tragic tale of the SS *Central America* also has an enormous factor in common with the story of the shipwreck of the *Tiger* (chapter 13): It would have far-reaching consequences, and once again would set off a disastrous chain of falling dominoes.

The Significance

Although she sank in 1857, the origin of the SS *Central America* story spans from 1848 to 1865, and involves the ruin of America's economy.

It would have a massively disruptive impact on her society and culture, and directly affect investors, banks, insurance companies, and one prominent treasure hunter. It would also involve the ghastly ruin of one ship and 426 human lives.

Perhaps even more significant than all of that, and having the largest and longest lasting impact, was that this single shipwreck—for the only time in US history—caused an unknown candidate from neither of the two main political parties to be elected as President of the United States. Incredibly, this was not even a third party; no third party has ever won. This was a fourth party, and it had only been formed six years earlier. Its platform unashamedly and unapologetically represented only the Northeast. Their candidate was a virtually unknown lawyer they portrayed as a "backwoods salt-of-the-earth," nicknamed "Honest." His name was Abraham Lincoln.

The Setting

America had been gradually expanding west since the Louisiana Purchase in 1803. This venture, however, was not for the faint of heart. It was an extremely rigorous, demanding, exhausting, and dangerous undertaking. It was only for the brave, the young, and the strong. It was likely that this appealed to those who had little reason to stay where they were, or those with nothing to lose, or those escaping something. The trip could easily take six months.

By 1850, a patient and wealthy traveler could go from the East Coast to the West Coast via a sailing or steam-powered ship.

Since the original Panama Canal did not open until 1914, a ship sailing from New York would have to go south for roughly 6,700 miles, round Cape Horn at the tip of South America, then sail north for another 7,200 miles to reach San Francisco. This took around two hundred days on average, but included many variables. Once again, this was a half-a-year commitment, not without its dangers and inconveniences, but certainly not as strenuous. One no longer needed to be young and strong—just rich.

SHIP TYPES IN THE 1800S

Clipper ship–Classic sailing ship of the nineteenth century, renowned for its beauty, grace, and speed. Apparently starting from the small, swift coastal packet known as the Baltimore clipper, the true clipper evolved first in American and later in British yards. In its ultimate form it was a long, slim, graceful vessel with a projecting bow and a radically streamlined hull, carrying an exceptionally large spread of sail on three tall masts. The emphasis on speed came partly from the desire to bring the first tea of the season back from China, and partly from competition with the overland route across North America to the California goldfields.

Paddle Wheel–Very popular ship in the 1800s designed by mounting the paddles in a wheel form, either at the stern or at the sides of the vessel. The device is highly efficient and is competitive even with modern propellers. It was supplanted by the latter because of the paddle wheel's vulnerability to damage in storms and its emergence from the water when the ship rolled heavily, which made steering difficult. For inland navigation these defects were insignificant, and paddle-wheel steamers long continued to operate on many rivers.

Steamship–Often referred to as a steamer, this is a type of steam-powered vessel, typically ocean-faring and seaworthy, that is propelled by one or more engines that heat water in boilers to produce the gas of steam, which typically drives propellers or paddle wheels, causing them to turn, thus providing propulsion.

California at this time was part of Mexico and sparsely settled. The population consisted of two extremes: Rugged trappers and hunters trading in the plentiful otter and beaver pelts was one extreme, and the other was rich rancheros. What became San Francisco began as a tent and shanty town in 1836, grew with the establishment of the Hudson Bay Company, but declined when that company left in 1846. By then, the population of two hundred was made up of mostly nomads, drifters, and deserting sailors.

Actual 1851 photograph of the incredibly busy San Francisco harbor and bustling town.
Public Domain

This all changed dramatically in 1848 when gold was discovered in Sutter's Mill, Coloma, California (forty-five miles east of Sacramento). The news quickly spread, and the 49ers (a nickname for the thousands who rushed to California for the gold in 1849) numbered four thousand by the following year. Soon it reached tens of thousands. One of the best lines to come out of the California Gold Rush of 1849 was "Never have so many worked so hard to not work!"

When the Mexican-American War ended in 1848, California became an American possession, with gold being the most obvious reason why. To that end, the US government subsidized private companies to build and operate two fleets of sidewheel paddle steamships. One fleet operated from California to Panama in the Pacific Ocean, the other from Panama to New York in the Atlantic Ocean. The idea was to efficiently connect the old US East Coast with the new US West Coast for news, mail, and passengers. The overwhelmingly obvious reason was simply to transport the huge volume of gold which was constantly pouring out of California to the US Treasury.

In her article, "Remembering Herndon's History: The SS *George Law*—The Life and Death of the Ship that Became the SS *Central America*," Barbara Glakas tells us:

> The US Mail Steamship Company was formed in 1848 by
> George Law, Marshall Roberts and Bowes McIlvaine. They
> retained a contract to carry US mail from New York to the Isth-
> mus of Panama, where it would then be delivered to California.
> The company also carried passengers. When the California Gold
> Rush began in the late 1840s, the company became very profit-
> able. In 1852, the company ordered two large ships to be built,
> one of which was ultimately named the SS *George Law*, after the
> New York financier and co-owner of the company.[1]

The Gold Route

The gold would leave San Francisco by paddlewheel steamship bound
for the Isthmus of Panama, around 3,300 nautical miles (or 2,900
statute miles). Everything was unloaded at docks in Panama City on
the Pacific Coast. Then, it was arduously transported the grueling fifty
miles through the jungle to the port of Aspinwall, now Colón, on the
Atlantic Coast.

ASPINWALL, PANAMA

Colón was founded as a result of the California Gold Rush. The city
began in 1850 as the starting point of a railroad line that carried people
across the Isthmus of Panama. The town was first named for William
Henry Aspinwall, who had built a shipping empire before focusing on the
California Gold Rush. In secret he developed plans to build a railroad
across the Isthmus of Panama to shorten the journey from coast to coast
by avoiding the perils of Cape Horn. In 1890, the name was changed to
Colón, the Spanish word for Columbus, to honor Christopher Columbus.

There the cargo was reloaded onto steamers of the Atlantic fleet bound for New York. This was made considerably easier when a railroad, started in 1850, was finally finished in 1855, at enormous cost in terms of money, energy, and human lives.

The Ship

Recall that the steamship SS *George Law* was previously mentioned with an explanation of its name. The SS *George Law* was a sidewheel paddler powered by a steam engine and also equipped with sails. Exact specifications were not kept then, but maritime expert Cedric Ridgely-Nevit tells us that "*George Law* measured about 271–278 feet, by 39–40 feet, by 30–32 feet. More current estimates put it at about 280 feet long. The tonnage was estimated to be 2,141 to 3,000 by carpenter's measure. The ship had one funnel and a pair of engines with a 65-inch bore and a 10-foot stroke. It had a wooden hull, was copper-sheathed and had three masts. Behind the front mast was the wheelhouse that featured a large double wheel. The galley was located directly in front of the stack."

The *Law* made her maiden voyage to Panama on October 20, 1853. She returned to New York on November 10, carrying 465 passengers and approximately $900,000 worth of California gold. That would be $24.45 million in today's dollars. An excellent start!

Law went on to a successful and regular service shared with the SS *Illinois*, sailing on the fifth and twentieth of every month. This continued until the *Law* was dry-docked in 1857. During that time her statistics were impressive: For each eight- or nine-day trip she carried between two hundred and eight hundred passengers and between $800,000 and $2 million in gold.

After forty-two profitable and successful voyages, the SS *George Law* was taken out of service for maintenance and upgrades.

Author Barbara Glakas explains:

> [The *Law*] was dry-docked back at the Webb Shipyard after her forty-second voyage. The engines were overhauled and some

of the hull's copper sheathing was replaced. It was during this dry-dock period in 1857 that the ship's name was changed to the SS *Central America*. It is unknown why the name change occurred—possibly to reflect its most common destination, and because George Law had sold his interest to his company back in 1853.[2]

Central America's Final Voyage

William Herndon, US Navy captain, departed the port of Aspinwall, Panama, on Thursday, September 3, 1857, bound for New York, but with a stop along the way. The SS *Central America* was carrying the now-usual 467 passengers, 102 crew members, and over 40,000 pounds of gold. (Once again, there are conflicting reports on the amount. Most have it at around twenty tons, or 40,000 pounds.) Several days later she docked in Havana, Cuba, for a routine stop. There, more passengers

J. Childs, author and publisher, 1857, rendering of the foundering SS Central America. *The panic, helplessness, and terror are readily conveyed by the artist. A potential rescuer, the brig* Marine, *is faintly seen in the background.*
Courtesy National Marine Museum, London

came aboard, among them Mr. H. H. Childs. The *Central America* departed on Tuesday, September 8, now bound directly for New York.

There are, of course, numerous written accounts of what happened on that fateful day of Saturday, September 12, 1857. None, however, is more original than the account by survivor Mr. H. H. Childs, who wrote an article published in the *Milwaukee Daily Sentinel* of September 22, 1857. The editor headlined the piece "Loss of the *Central America*: Further Particulars of the Disaster."

In the article Childs reports that "The weather was delightful and the sea calm" that day. However, "On the following morning [Friday, September 11, a] storm raged fearfully."[3] Actually, the *Central America* had found itself in the fury of a hurricane, the kind for which the Graveyard of the Atlantic is famous. The *Central America* began taking on water. The violent waves rocked the ship unmercifully, making it virtually impossible to feed coal into the hungry boilers; thus, she was quickly losing power. A bucket brigade of men was quickly formed, and they bailed furiously.

By just after noon on Saturday, the fate of the *Central America* appeared to be hopeless. Fortunately, a ship was seen on the horizon. It was the brig *Marine*, drawing closer to help. Captain Herndon of the *Central America* ordered women and children on deck to facilitate

Captain Herndon of the SS Central America *arranged for some women and children to be safely transferred to the* Marine. *In Thomas C. Reeves's 1975 book,* Gentleman Boss, *he relates the following: "Survivors of the disaster reported last seeing Commander Herndon in full uniform, standing by the wheelhouse with his hand on the rail, hat off and in his hand, with his head bowed in prayer as the ship gave a lurch and went down. Herndon's concern for his passengers and crew helped save 152 of the 575 people on board."*
Public Domain

boarding the lifeboats, and some were safely transferred to the *Marine*. Unfortunately, due to the rough seas, the *Marine* drifted away and was unable to help further.

A few minutes past eight p.m. a tremendous and terrifying rogue wave completely engulfed the *Central America*, sinking it immediately.

Childs continues, "I think some four hundred or four hundred and fifty souls were launched upon the ocean at the mercy of the waves." He chronicles the fact that for several hours the group floated helplessly and silently. Then, "I saw my comrades sink fast, and at one o'clock that night I was nearly alone upon the ocean, some two hundred miles from land."[4]

A total of 425 (some accounts say 426) passengers and crew lost their lives in this maritime disaster. And let's not forget about the forty thousand pounds of gold that also went down.

Significance and Consequences

"When news came through the telegraph wires that the ship had sunk off the coast of North Carolina, the country went into a panic. It was a time when the country relied on gold to back its banking transactions. Banks closed, businesses went bankrupt and the financial Panic of 1857 deepened—all because the much-awaited Ship of Gold had disappeared with tons of needed gold on board,"[5] reports Mike Fuljenz.

According to the Monaco Rare Coins website: "The 'Ship of Gold' sank in deep water off the coast of the Carolinas. The loss has been described as the greatest economic catastrophe in all of US maritime history, triggering the Panic of 1857, a severe recession and a deep depression."

Writer Sean Munger notes: "It was one of the worst maritime disasters of the nineteenth century. The ripple effect of the *Central America* sinking went far beyond the loss of the ship and its crew, however. The 40,000 pounds of gold aboard the *Central America* was equal to about 20 percent of all the gold held in New York banks at the time. This was an era when the currency system was not regulated by the federal

AFTERSHOCKS—
THE FIRST "BLACK FRIDAY"

The first Black Friday in US history occurred on September 24, 1869, when plummeting gold prices triggered a securities market panic. The crash was caused by an attempt by financier Jay Gould and railway magnate James Fisk to corner the gold market and drive up the price.

government, and thus was subject to highly dangerous fluctuations, speculation, runs, and other financial hazards."[6]

Problems multiplied. "In September 1857, Ohio Life Insurance and Trust Company—a major banking institution based in New York—collapsed, and rumors of embezzlement were rife. The ensuing panic led to many customers trying to withdraw their money from other banks. For this reason, a particularly large cargo of an estimated 30,000 pounds of gold was dispatched from the San Francisco Mint to shore up eastern banks."[7]

The tragic shipwreck of SS *Central America* was a prime catalyst to the following major developments. The climate of the times in the America of 1857 was not a good one. We were very close to becoming the Divided States of America. The country now had three distinct sections: the Northeast, the Deep South, and the West. Each section had its own society, with separate culture and politics.

The South had three distinct societies—the wealthy plantation owners (derived mostly from British high society); the middle class of simple farmers, shopkeepers, and laborers; and the poor African slaves. More than half of the US presidents by then had come from the South. The agrarian area relied on excellent trade relations with England for their high-quality manufactured goods. The pace of life there was relaxed and genteel. They were "outside people" at ease with nature. Transportation was by horse, carriage, and steamboat.

The Northeast at this time was highly industrialized. Factory cities had become large, dirty, and unruly, the population mainly derived from poor European countries such as Ireland, Poland, Czechoslovakia,

Germany, and the like. Most of these poor immigrants, looking for a fresh start in the "land of opportunity," became laborers in the factories and sweat shops. The hours were long, pay was low, and the conditions were highly dangerous. These workers often lived in crowded and unkempt slums. The pace of life was fast and often unfriendly, simply due to congestion. These were "inside people," dealing mostly with their urban, man-made surroundings. Transportation was by city streets, paved turnpikes, plank roads, canals, and railroads. The very small upper class, of course, was made up of factory and business owners. The Northeast was the financial center of the nation and thus controlled much of America's economy.

The West was yet again entirely different from these other two cultures. It was wild! Attracted to this naked freedom were loners, wanderers, and those down-and-out who had nothing to gain from where they had been living. They were nobody's slaves, nobody's subordinate worker bees. They were free and independent, setting off on their own. They would run their own lives, earn their own livelihood, and live by their own laws. Many preferred that there be *no* laws! There was also a great and steady conflict with the Native Americans inhabiting these territories. The West could not care less about the North or the South. Everyone was more or less the same class. They were extremely independent and capable of "living off the land." Transportation was over dusty cattle and Indian trails by horse or wagon. Rivers were also utilized where available.

Adding to this economic instability and the social and cultural diversity and friction of sectionalism was political instability. The presidential election following the Panic of 1857 came only three years later. Many divisive and negative events would lead up to this: the Missouri Compromise, reversed later by the Kansas-Nebraska Act (affecting the critical balance of slave versus free states); tariff issues which benefited the North and hurt the South; the polarizing US Supreme Court "*Dred Scott* Decision" that declared slaves to be property, with no rights; and finally capped off by the murderous and terrorist act of John Brown's Raid in Virginia only a year before the election. Brown's attempt to arm the slaves for a violent insurrection alarmed both the North and the South.

This divided country naturally produced divided political parties. The old Whig Party which started in 1833 and had links to the Federalist Party had virtually disappeared. It now formed briefly again as the Constitutional Union Party, nominating John Bell for president and espousing a neutral platform that didn't favor any particular section. The Democratic Party, evolving from Thomas Jefferson, had now split into Northern and Southern groups. The Southern Democrats nominated John C. Breckinridge and stood for protecting the slave-based Southern economy. The Northern Democrats nominated Stephen A. Douglas and advocated "popular sovereignty," meaning "Let the people decide." A brand-new party, named the Republican Party, was formed as recently as 1854, only six years prior to the election, in order to take advantage of the Democratic Party split. They nominated a virtually unknown lawyer, Abraham Lincoln, born in the backwoods of Kentucky but now practicing in Illinois.

Since this new party had nothing to lose, their platform was unabashedly and solely pro-Northern. They favored high tariffs and promoted the construction of canals and railroads which only served the industrial North. They opposed slavery, and as an enticement to get more votes, they blatantly offered free land to settlers of the Western territories.

Due to the overwhelming population of the North—22.8 million, versus 5.5 million in the South—and by splitting the strength of the Democratic Party in half, the new Republicans won the election. Clearly, they did not stand for the United States, but only for the Northeast. The South had little choice but to form their own country, for much of the same reasons that the American colonists had earlier declared their independence from Great Britain.

Many of those divisions, scars, and sectional rivalries remain in our country today, more than a century and a half later. The tragic shipwreck of SS *Central America* unwittingly was a prime catalyst to these developments.

CHAPTER 22

NUOVA OTTAVIA

The dramatic sunset taking place at the time of this wreck highlighted what the record says was a "melancholy disaster." The botched rescue attempt of this Italian bark makes no sense, except for being a series of fatal novice mistakes.

The wreck and subsequent failed rescue of the Italian bark *Nuova Ottavia* on March 1, 1876, on the Currituck Beaches was an unnecessary and quite avoidable tragedy. This occurred during the period of cronyism before the total reorganization of the Life-Saving Service in 1878 (see "The Phoenix Arises" section in chapter 20). This proved to be unfortunate for all involved.

Although this chapter is included in the "Dramatic Failures" section, it just as easily could have been included in "The Mysterious" section, as it contains several unknowns and unanswered questions.

North Carolina's well-known lighthouses are famous and beloved. The Currituck Beach Lighthouse of 1875, located in the village of Corolla, was the last one built on the stretch from Hatteras Island, Bodie, and Currituck Beach (more were to be built elsewhere on the North Carolina coast).

These lighthouses were revered, romanticized, and celebrated as sentinels of the sea, saving countless lives with their steady warnings. When the inevitable shipwrecks did occur, however, the little-known but vastly important US Life-Saving Service was there. The Jones

North Carolina lighthouse expert and artist John Havel's conception of the construction of the Currituck Beach Lighthouse.
Courtesy John Havel

Hill Life-Saving Station was one of the very first built on the North Carolina coast, and one of seven in a series begun in 1874. It was in Corolla, later renamed "Whales Head," and finally changed to "Currituck Beach."

By the spring of 1876, the Currituck Beach Lighthouse was nearly completed. It was officially commissioned on December 1, 1875, but as with any major construction project, there were still details that needed attention. Important to this story are two of the personnel who worked there: H. T. Halstead, a clerk at the lighthouse, and George W. Wilson, one of the laborers.

CURRITUCK BEACH LIGHTHOUSE

North Carolina's modern lighthouses began with Cape Lookout in 1859. The design of red brick with black ironwork was so successful that it was used with only slight modifications for the next three. In order of time and geography of south to north, those are the Cape Hatteras Lighthouse in Buxton (1870), Bodie Island Lighthouse in South Nags Head (1872), and finally, Currituck Beach Lighthouse in Corolla (1875). The problem then arose that along North Carolina's low-lying and largely indistinguishable coast were four redbrick lighthouses with black ironwork and nearly identical shapes. So, a distinguishable black-and-white paint scheme was initiated. Cape Lookout would have a double-helix design resulting in diamond shapes; Cape Hatteras would have the famous "barber-pole" stripes; Bodie Island would have two horizontal black-and-white stripes; and Currituck would be distinguished by being the only one that was unpainted. These became the invaluable "day marks" for navigators.

The Currituck Beach Lighthouse is located thirty-four miles south of Cape Henry, Virginia, and is thirty-two miles north of Bodie Island, North Carolina. It is 162 feet to the top, requiring a climb of 214 steps, and its beacon is visible for eighteen nautical miles.

It is worth noting that the United States officially referred to the structure not as a "lighthouse" but rather as a "light station." The reason it was not named the "Corolla Lighthouse" was because the structures were named for the beach or geographical area on which they were located, not the village they were in. It would be just as incorrect to refer to the Cape Hatteras Lighthouse as "the Buxton Light."

A mile north of this lighthouse, the Jones Hill LSS Station (eventually called "Currituck Beach") had been completed in late 1874. All stations in the Service at this time were only open and operational during what they called "the storm season" of December through March. This meant the lifesavers at this new station had worked and trained—at the most—four months in 1874–1875 and another four months in 1876. They were clearly an inexperienced crew, and due to the nature of the Service at that time, we really don't know how qualified they were or how much real training they had actually received.

The Ship

Little is known about the *Nuova Ottavia*. She was an Italian bark that sailed from Genoa, Italy, to Baltimore, Maryland, "in ballast." On board were Captain Bozzo, his wife and child, and a crew of twelve.

SOME NAUTICAL TERMS

Bark—A sailing ship with three or more masts. The foremast was square-rigged and the aftermast was rigged fore and aft.

Rigging—The system of ropes, cables, and chains, which support a sailing ship or sailboat's masts—standing rigging, non-moving bracing—the running rigging, lines, and pulleys that move.

In ballast—Sailing empty in order to pick up cargo, or just having deposited cargo.

Yard—The horizontal spar at 90 degrees to the masts that carries the sail. The term *yardarm*—which refers only to the tip or end of the yard—is often misused.

Clew up—To retract the sail to the yard; "clew down" is to release or set the sail from the yard.

The Wreck

The records of Jones Hill LSS Station reported that the bark *Nuova Ottavia* had been seen around sunset on Wednesday evening, March 1, 1876. The report stated that it was about five miles from shore with rough seas and "rather high and heavy surf," as well as a strong southeast wind. Soon after dark, the bark was seen to be "stranded on the reef" (which local reports would call the "bar," or sandbar). It was totally unclear to all witnesses at this time how or why this had happened. Especially puzzling was the fact that all her sails were set, "not even clewed up," and remained so all night. This is clearly not the correct nautical procedure for these circumstances, so another "why" question remains unanswered.

A crowd had gathered on the beach as the surfboat was dragged out on its cart by the lifesaving crew. Some were villagers and some were from the nearby lighthouse.

All sources agree on what happened next.

Although it was dark by 7:20 p.m., and the bark lay just four hundred yards offshore, well within reach of the Lyle gun, the keeper and crew launched the surfboat. This was yet another major mystery, compounded by the fact that none of the surfmen donned the only safety device they had—cork life belts.

A typical depiction of a crew from the USLSS on the Atlantic Coast launching a surfboat in heavy surf—the most dangerous part of the entire ocean. These surfmen are wearing their cork life belts.
Courtesy US Coast Guard

One of the six surfmen was absent, having previously been sent off to retrieve supplies. The lighthouse clerk, Mr. H. T. Halstead, stepped into the boat, volunteering to replace the missing surfman. He even manned an oar. Quickly, however, laborer George W. Wilson insisted that he was younger and stronger, and so he took over the volunteer place.

The crowd on the beach watched the surfboat successfully negotiate the initial breakers, the hardest and most dangerous part of the launch. They watched the small lantern light at the rear of the boat bob up and down as it was battered by the rough surf, until it went out of sight. Suddenly, a terrifying scream was heard back on the beach. Then silence.

The shocked crowd was stunned shortly thereafter to see something wash ashore. According to author David Stick, "A constant watch was kept on the beach then, and soon after one of the lifeboat oars drifted ashore, then a second, a third, and a fourth. After that the boat itself, turned bottom upwards, empty; and still later, one of the lifesavers, Malachi Brurmsey, all life gone from his body."[1] Throughout the night the crowd made up of family, friends, and neighbors watched, wondered, and worried.

At dawn, the mystery deepened. The bark was still there, sails flapping. Eight men were counted standing on the deck in desperate need of rescue. But who was there to do it?

The nightmare unfolded as one by one the bodies of Keeper John G. Gale; surfmen Lemuel Griggs, Lewis White, Spencer D. Gray, and volunteer George Wilson; and five unidentified Italian sailors washed ashore. From the USLSS Annual Report that year: "The bodies of the keeper and crew of this station (No. 4) thus found were delivered to their respective families for interment, and those of the five Italians were buried about three hundred yards north of the station."[2] One of the surfmen, Jeremiah Munden, was still unaccounted for. Sadly, he was not found until two weeks later. He was buried respectfully nearby at Paul Gamiels Hill. Munden was African-American, part of what the Service commonly called "checkerboard crews," composed of black and white crew members.

He became the first African American to lose his life in the course of duty to the LSS. Amazingly, the loss of this entire crew in 1876 represented the first losses of surfmen on duty since the USLSS had begun nationally in 1871.

Chaos Reigns

Eight people visible from shore remained on the ship. Who were they? They had been in range of the Lyle gun all along, which dutifully had been carried to the wreck scene. There was plenty of shot, powder, and all apparatus necessary to set up the necessary breeches buoy. Tragically, now there was no one who had the experience to operate all of this. Nevertheless, the crowd on the beach tried. They fired the Lyle gun. Stick writes, "They fired time after time after time, until the shot was exhausted and the vent in the mortar was clogged by sand. Forty-one rockets were sent up throughout the day and night, as encouragement for the men stranded on the vessel."[3]

By two p.m. the next day the *Nuova Ottavia* had been battered into so many pieces that she simply disappeared. One large section of the stern had come ashore near Kitty Hawk, twenty miles farther south.

As a curtain call, four Italian sailors were finally retrieved from the surf, clinging to a piece of wreckage. They were exhausted and barely alive.

What Happened

As with so many of these mysteries, we not only don't know what really happened, but there is also conflicting information. In testimony to a subsequent investigation, the four Italian sailors said this is what happened. As noted in the same Annual Report: "The [surf]boat pulled entirely around the vessel when she first went off, and finally secured a line on the lee side. Holding on this line with a considerable scope brought the boat under the bows of the bark where the sea was curling around, which partially rebounding, filled her. The line thus made fast was the whip, which with the No. 2 grapnel, one boat and one house lantern, one water and one fire bucket were lost from the boat, which afterward came onshore bottom upward."[4]

To the contrary, author Joe A. Mobley reports in his book, *Ship Ashore!: The US Lifesavers of Coastal North Carolina*: "The events of that fateful night are not entirely certain, but at some point in the rescue attempt, the surfboat overturned and Gale, three surfmen, and five Italian sailors drowned. The subsequent prevailing opinion held that the boat became swamped when the Italians in panic tried to board it 'in a mob as soon as the surfboat came to the wreck.'"[5]

The disaster left many lingering, troubling, unanswered questions, including "Why had the *Nuova Ottavia* grounded where it did?" and "Why weren't the cork life belts used?" and "Why was the Lyle gun not used by the surfmen?" (It was only used afterward by civilians).

The Consequences

Since this was the first loss of lives for the Service—and a full crew at that—conducting a thorough investigation was of the utmost importance. The report found three major faults: 1) The cork life belts were not used; 2) The keeper probably chose the wrong lifesaving equipment; and 3) Depending on the surf and wind conditions, even though the breeches buoy would have been slower than the surfboat, it would have been easier and more effective in the long run; but this would have been dependent on the expertise and judgment of an experienced keeper at the time.

The Service sternly issued the following orders: 1) All surfmen must wear cork life belts before entering the surfboat; and 2) The station keeper is charged with seeing that every surfman at the station has a cork life belt in good condition.

Unfortunately, it was not possible to answer the most important question of what had actually happened that night. Without knowing the details, there could be no solution. It did lead to some obvious necessary improvements, such as better training for all surfmen and keepers, as well as mandatory use of life belts. Although not required, it is now strongly urged that crews contact neighboring stations to assist if needed. Finally, in order to avoid the victims panicking and swamping the surfboat, the keeper must maintain rigid authority and discipline by completely taking charge of the situation in a calm manner.

In concluding their document, the Annual Report said, "It is gratifying to acknowledge the receipt of $408 in gold (over $11,000 in today's dollars) for the families of the lifesavers on behalf of the Italian Society of Salvage."[6] It is documented in the *Congressional Record* of that year that a Mr. Cox noted, "To that committee was referred a bill to relieve the widows of the gallant men that went down beneath the breakers on the North Carolina coast in attempting to save Italian strangers." Concluding his remarks, Mr. Cox eloquently said, "Their noble efforts to rescue the shipwreck sailors shed a luster over the victims and a credit on humanity."

The bill passed, granting Keeper Gale's family $78 ($1,837 in today's dollars), and $55 ($1,295 in today's dollars) for each surfman's family.

As is so often the case, some lessons had not been learned. There would be more shipwrecks. There would be more loss of life among sailors, passengers, and surfmen. Then there would be the *Huron* and the *Metropolis*.

CHAPTER 23
STRATHAIRLY

The wreck of the Strathairly *is a heartbreaking saga of rescuers being on the scene yet powerless to help the victims because of rough seas and an extremely heavy fog. Poor conditions thwarted numerous rescue attempts for more than twelve hours. Nineteen of the twenty-six crew were lost, their bodies found more than a mile away.*

Coming Full Circle

Our opening shipwreck story took place at the Chicamacomico Life-Saving Station in Rodanthe. It was an incredibly heroic and amazingly successful event, against all odds—and there were plenty of odds.

Our final shipwreck story also took place at Chicamacomico, but shows the flip side of the coin. It was a dreadful, very painful failure, and not because the heroes failed; rather, it shows that there were times when, in spite of all their selfless efforts, their training and unwavering determination, and their dogged persistence, the lifesavers simply could not overcome insurmountable obstacles.

That was the case with the *Strathairly*.

At the time of this photo, the Chicamacomico LSS complex, which had responded to the Strathairly's *calls for help, had been long abandoned.*
Courtesy US Coast Guard

The Basics

According to the USLSS Annual Report for that year, "One of the most disastrous wrecks in the history of Hatteras Island was that of the 1,236-ton schooner-rigged screw steamer *Strathairly*, which stranded a mile and a quarter south of Chicamacomico Station, March 24, 1891. Nineteen of the crew of twenty-six were lost within sight of the shore, and only seven were miraculously saved."[1]

The Ship

To the ears of English-speaking people, *Strathairly* is an awkward-sounding name. That is because it is not English—it is Gaelic. Conducting casual reading or light research on the British ship *Strathairly* can be very confusing indeed. Here is why: The one in our story was built in 1876 by Sir Rayleton Dixon and Company at the Cleveland Dockyard in Middlesbrough-on-Tees. The River Tees and the town of

MORE NAUTICAL VOCABULARY

Bar—Most of the North Carolina coast has two sandbars running parallel to the beach, separated by a hundred yards or more, thus creating an "inner bar" and an "outer bar."

Semaphore—Any device used for visual signaling.

Powder—"Black powder" or gunpowder; a mixture of sulfur (S), charcoal (C), and potassium nitrate (saltpeter, KNO3). The charcoal makes it black.

Forecastle—The forward "castle," an archaic term for raised deck; eventually corrupted to "fo'csle" (pronounced FOLK-sul).

Homogeneous cargoes—The ones most often carried by tramp steamers. This would be an entire hold of a single commodity, such as coal, iron, lumber, sugar, ice, rum, chalk, etc.

Nautical mile—A unit of measurement used in both air and marine navigation, and for the definition of territorial waters. Historically, it was defined as one minute of a degree of latitude. Today it is defined as exactly 1,852 meters (equivalent to 1.15 statute miles). The derived unit of speed is the *knot*, one nautical mile per hour.

Line vs. rope—When the item is unused, it is coiled or wound on something for storage and called "rope." When it is employed for use on a ship, it forms a functioning line and is thus referred to as a "line." Each line on a ship has a name, such as "sheet," "clew," and "halyard." Thus, the first job a new sailor has is "to learn the ropes."

Bent—Past tense of "to bend," meaning to fasten or attach; to secure by hitching or tying a knot.

Littoral current—The flow of current parallel to the shore. This is why you end up farther down the beach from where you entered the ocean.

Middlesbrough are in Yorkshire, England. The Dixon Company existed from 1862 until 1923. It had built over six hundred ships, including passenger and cargo steamers as well as naval warships. It was the largest shipbuilder on the River Tees.

MIDDLESBROUGH

In 1850, ironstone was discovered in Middlesbrough, quickly becoming the economic lifeblood of the town. The importance of pig-iron production was great enough to give rise to the town's nickname of "Ironopolis." It was therefore a natural location for shipyards building iron and steel ships.

However, the Strath Steamship Mutual Insurance Association had formed earlier in Scotland. The Scottish (or Gaelic) word *Strath* translates as "broad mountain valley." It is a common prefix, just as *loch* is Gaelic for "lake" (as in Loch Ness). Consequently, there were dozens of ships actually named *Strathairly* in Scotland. "Airly" (also Airlie) was an old family name; there is even an Airly Castle in Angus, Scotland. There are many more English/Scottish ships with the prefix "Strath."

Our 1891 SS *Strathairly* was a schooner-rigged screw steamer. This simply means she had masts and sails in the schooner designation (see first sidebar in chapter 6 for definition of "schooner"), and that she was powered by steam engines which drove screw-type propellers. Here again, another of our cherished and long-believed misconceptions is upset: "SS" does not mean "Steam Ship," but rather "Screw Steamer."

Our *Strathairly* was a large tramp steamer, at 1,236 tons register, with a crew of twenty-six and a cargo of iron ore obtained in Santiago, Cuba, bound for Baltimore, Maryland. A tramp steamer is a merchant ship that operates without a schedule, going wherever required to deliver its cargoes. The tramp is a descendant of the early merchant ships, whose masters (also their owners) loaded them with cargo at home to sell abroad, and vice versa. Tramps are used mainly for carrying bulk commodities or homogeneous cargoes in whole shiploads, with each voyage separately negotiated between the ship's owner and the shipper, usually through a broker.[2] A tramp steamer is to the waters what a street vendor with a cart is to city streets.

On this voyage, the steamer was commanded by Captain William Wynne of North Shields, Tyne Wear County, England. By 1871, our

MARYLAND FOUNDRIES

Very early in the history of the colony of Maryland, iron ore was discovered in the Arundel ore belt. This quickly gave rise to smelting furnaces, blacksmith shops, foundries, and eventually, to shipbuilding. With its location on the Patapsco River, Baltimore was an ideal place for shipbuilding yards and companies. The river empties directly into the vast Chesapeake Bay, which in turn is the gateway to the Atlantic Ocean and the East Coast of the United States. The bonus of being located in the heart of iron country made Maryland the leading shipbuilder in the nation by 1790.

Strathairly was fifteen years old, a somewhat tired workhorse that had carried large and heavy loads over hundreds of thousands of nautical miles. Nevertheless, she did not deserve this end.

The Wreck

Around 4:40 a.m. on Tuesday, March 24, 1891, the British tramp steamer SS *Strathairly* ran hard aground on Hatteras Island, at the center of the infamous Graveyard of the Atlantic. This was a mile and a quarter south of the Chicamacomico Station in the village of Rodanthe. It was high tide on that cold and blustery morning. There was a strong northeast wind with a heavy surf breaking on the shore—so heavy the surfboats could not be launched. The single worst ingredient in this fatal recipe, however, was the extremely dense fog hanging over the sands and surf, which locals referred to as "smoke on the water" conditions.

Strathairly had grounded four or five hundred yards from the beach on the outer bar and was within reasonable Lyle gun range to employ the beach apparatus and the breeches buoy. The paramount problem was that the fog-shrouded ship could not be seen. It immediately sounded a distress signal with its steam whistle. Just as quickly, it was answered by a Coston flare from the Chicamacomico surfmen on beach patrol, heading south toward the Gull Shoal Station.

SIX OF THE CREW SAVED.

Thick Weather Caused the Wreck of the Straithairly.

ELIZABETH CITY, N. C., March 26.—[Special]—Lieut. Failing, of the life-saving service, who is at the wreck of the British steamer Straithairly, reports the following saved: R. Turner, second officer; Geo. Simpson, boatswain; Albert Smith, seaman; John W. Halon, ordinary seaman; William McArthur, fireman; John Campbell, fireman.

The reason assigned by the survivors for the wreck was thick weather and inability to take observations.

The men saved are thoroughly exhausted from exposure and are unable to travel and are in bad condition. The men will arrive in Elizabeth City Saturday. The vessel struck at 4:40 Tuesday morning, and before daylight had gone to pieces. The captain and navigator had been on the bridge for three days and nights and, being unable to get an observation, recorded himself at Bodies Island. The life saving crews succeeded in getting a line to the vessel, but the men on board were so benumbed by exposure that they were unable to

Newspaper account of the wreck and tragic rescue attempts of the Straithairly *by the Chicamacomico crew (*Roanoke Times, *March 26, 1891).*
Public Domain

COMMUNICATING BY COLOR

Twenty-six-year-old Benjamin Franklin Coston was a promising inventor for the US Navy. He had been experimenting with color-coded night signals to allow communication between ships, but died suddenly before completing his work. His twenty-one-year-old wife Martha was determined to finish his work, and did so, in 1859. She explained the invention this way: "This is a very ingenious and effective semaphore, which commends itself from its simplicity. Three lights of different colors, white, red, and green, are so flashed or burned in combinations representing the numerals 1, 2, 3, 4, 5, 6, 7, 8, 9, 0, and also two letters, A and P (for time of day, a.m. or p.m.)—in all twelve combinations. The light is produced by the combustion of a peculiar pyrotechnic composition for each of the desired colors. A handle or holder is all that is necessary, ordinarily, to hold the selected color." (http://www.civilwarsignals.org/pages/signal/signalpages/flare/coston.html)

It eventually became standard operating procedure that when a wreck occurred, the responding station would immediately contact its neighboring stations. With few exceptions, every USLSS station on the North Carolina coast had one neighboring station to the north, referred to as their "sister station," and one to the south, referred to as their "brother station."

This is exactly what Chicamacomico Station Keeper Josiah Holly Wescott did. Very soon, three stations were present at the wreck scene. Keeper Pugh and his Gull Shoal crew were the first to arrive; then from farther north came Keeper John Allen Midgett Sr.'s crew of the New Inlet Station. Like all stations that responded, they provided valuable reserves of trained lifesavers, boats, beach apparatus, and extra supplies of powder, shot, and lines. As a hallmark of the Service, this provided a shot of adrenaline of teamwork, brotherhood, and camaraderie. Added to this contingent of those wanting to assist were villagers and Lieutenant Failing, the USLSS district inspector. He was fortunately nearby on a regular tour of inspection and was staying on the vessel *Alert*, lying in the Pamlico Sound. He was not only able to witness the event, but also to submit a personal report.

The following direct quotes are from his record. The lieutenant initially reported that "Survivors heard a gun fired abreast of the wreck in less than half an hour" after arriving. Although the ship could not be seen, the whistle and voices of the men could be clearly heard. The lifesavers had a fairly good guess as to the distance. What they did not know at this time, however, was that the *Strathairly*'s lifeboats had immediately been smashed or washed away upon launching. Therefore, the breeches buoy would be the singular source of their salvation.

Thus, "The crew then took to the rigging, as the sea was breaking completely over the vessel . . . Very shortly after this the steamer commenced breaking in two. About daybreak, the main mast fell over the side and took with it [those who had climbed up it], the captain, first officer, and chief engineer, who were lost."

The fog had finally lifted enough around ten a.m. so that the ship could be seen by three crews of lifesavers and the people of nearby villages. It was now six hours since the wreck. Preparations for the rescue began.

The Lyle gun could be loaded with a black-powder charge varying from one to eight ounces, depending on the range to the target. The first shot toward the visible *Strathairly* had a charge of six ounces, with a medium-size No. 7 shot line attached. It fell short. The next shot used the smaller and lighter No. 4 line in hopes of increasing distance. It worked, as the shot actually landed on the fo'csle. Since this line was so small, the larger and stronger No. 9 line was "bent" (or attached) to the No. 4 line. The lifesavers then used that to send out to the ship, but within a few yards of the vessel, it broke.

SHOT LINES

There were only three different size lines: No. 4, No. 7, and No. 9. This referred to the diameter of each line: $4/32$ of an inch, $7/32$, and $9/32$.

"Being prepared for such a contingency," Lieutenant Failing continued, "no time was lost by the Station men, the next shot carrying a No.
7 line . . . with a powder charge of eight ounces." This shot also successfully landed on the ship. The earlier procedure was then repeated—
unfortunately with the same broken-line results. They fired again and
the No. 7 line broke again. "In this way, effort after effort was made to
send the gear off until three o'clock in the afternoon, the gun being fired
as fast as lines could be faked down."

By now, something else was not making sense. At this point the
lifesavers knew that at least five of the shots had successfully landed, yet
there was no reaction on board the ship. This part of the breeches-buoy
rescue was always dependent on a sailor on board the ship to haul in the
shot line, which began the entire process (see chapter 1).

The lifesavers, consumed with their intense work, finally noticed that
they could only see two or three at work on the deck. The only surviving officer, the second mate, later explained that all the remaining crew
except three were too exhausted and "benumbed and helpless from
exposure" to be of any help.

Eight hours into this disaster, around noon, seaman Albert Smith, at
his wits' end, donned a life belt and jumped overboard; "after a desperate struggle in the surf, [Smith] was pulled out by the surfmen, uncon-
scious and nearly dead." He was brought to the house of former keeper
John Allen Midgett because it was closer than the station.

Now, around five o'clock, everyone was twelve hours into this cruel
and grueling incident. In utter desperation, the remaining *Strathairly*
sailors shouted to the lifesavers that they also were jumping in with life
belts, hoping to swim ashore. Immediately, however, the strong littoral
currents swept them rapidly southward, parallel to but not heading
toward the beach. Lieutenant Failing reported, "The surfmen and the
inhabitants of the neighboring settlements [North Rodanthe, South
Rodanthe (now Waves), and Salvo], many of whom had been present
on the beach all day, at once followed them, and at great risk to themselves, in wading out into the surf, succeeded in dragging sixteen men
out of the water."

Unfortunately, this extreme bravery only led to finding ten of them already dead, even though "immediate efforts were made to resuscitate them, but without avail." Almost apocalyptically, twenty minutes later, all remains of the battered *Strathairly* disappeared into the writhing and swirling sea. All seven of the survivors eventually made it to the Chicamacomico Station, "where they were taken to comfortable quarters in the station . . . [and] provided with dry clothing from the supply donated by the Women's National Relief Association. The ten bodies taken out of the surf were carried to the station, placed in boxes made by the life saving [*sic*] men, a minister was sent for, and they were buried on the morning of the 26th near the station."

In their day, the men of the US Life-Saving Service all over the nation routinely made daring, dramatic, and dangerous rescues. Time after time they accomplished the near-impossible at great risk to themselves, "so that others may live." They usually faced conditions, like today's first responders, where they found themselves running in when everyone else was running out. Almost always, they found ways to surmount the insurmountable.

But not always.

The *Strathairly*'s surviving crew composed a letter of thanks for the men and women who had risked their lives during the rescue attempt.

Note: A Letter of Thanks

CHICAMICOMICO [*sic*] STATION

March 26, 1891

DEAR SIR:

We wish to express our heartfelt thanks to the keepers and crews of Chicamicomico [*sic*], Gull Shoal, and New Inlet stations for the brave and noble service rendered to us by them on March 24, in rescuing us from the surf, as it was impossible for us to gain a footing in our exhausted condition; also for the kind attention we received at their quarters; and we also thank the Women's National Relief Association for the clothing we received, as we were utterly destitute of clothing.

Expressions of thanks are but a feeble return for such services, but we hope they will be accepted and prove a source of encouragement to the noble workers in future times of peril.

Most respectfully, we remain yours,

R. TURNER, Second Officer; G. SIMPSON, Boatswain; W. McARTHUR; J. CAMPBELL; ALBERT SMITH; JOHN WALER; and C. NORTHCOTE

CONCLUSION

A BRIEF LOOK AT ALL TWENTY-NINE NORTH CAROLINA USLSS STATIONS

I was teaching North Carolina history in Durham, North Carolina, when I had an interview for the principalship of the Ocracoke School on the Outer Banks. On the way down Hatteras Island, I was attracted to an old, seemingly deserted, and dilapidated building. I stopped and gazed at it, and was mesmerized. I had no idea what it was. My own voice inside my head said, "I have got to help this place." Never before or since have I had such an experience.

The building was the Chicamacomico Life-Saving Station. Fifteen years later, I was the site manager of a now-thriving historic attraction. I did help that place, and in the process, my interest in the stunning history of this incredible, almost forgotten, Service was sparked.

While this book relates stories about particular stations, wrecks, and rescues, I would be remiss if I ignored the remainder. Space limitations require only brief glimpses of those additional stations.

The eventual twenty-nine North Carolina US Life-Saving Service Stations are listed here geographically, from north to south.

Dates in parenthesis indicate date beginning of operations for the first station, and then, if there was one, the newer, rebuilt (often replacement) station.

Wash Woods (1878, 1933)

Location: On beach abreast Knotts Island, Deals. Once called Deal's Island Station. Early station once used as a dance hall. Subsequent station now a private home.

Total Wrecks

Schooner *Arleville H. Peary* on October 31, 1908.
Became waterlogged and drifted ashore two and a half miles south of False Cape Station (VA) and two and a quarter miles north of Wash Woods Station. Her distress signal was discovered by the patrols from both stations, who burned a Coston in response and gave the alarm. The Wash Woods crew hauled their apparatus to a point on the beach abreast of the wreck, where they were met by the surfmen from the False Cape Station. The first shot line went beyond the reach of the imperiled seamen, but a second line landed directly on the schooner's cabin. The whip and hawser were then hauled off with little difficulty, and the crew of six men was taken off. By this time the boat wagon from the False Cape Station had arrived and the lifesavers went aboard the schooner for the men's clothing and personal effects. The shipwrecked crew was cared for at the Wash Woods Station until November 3, when they were furnished transportation to Knotts Island to obtain passage to Norfolk. The schooner was a total loss.[1]

Schooner *John S. Wood* on April 7, 1889; zero lives lost.
Schooner *Henry P. Simmons* on October 23, 1889; seven lives lost.
Bark *Clythia* on January 22, 1894; zero lives lost.
Schooner *Mabel Rose* on October 11, 1903; zero lives lost.

Pennys Hill (1878)

Location: Five and three-quarter miles north of Currituck Beach Lighthouse, Corolla. Old station recently moved to original site six and a half miles north of Corolla for use as private home. Once called Old Currituck Inlet.

See also "Barkentine *Samuel Welsh*" in next section.

Currituck Beach (1874, 1903)

Location: About one mile north of Currituck Lighthouse, Corolla, NC 12. Also called Jones Hill. Later station also recently moved from original location in Corolla to site adjacent to Pennys Hill Station for use as private home.

Total Wrecks

Brig *Annie McFarland* on January 30, 1873; zero lives lost.

Bark *Nuova Ottavia* on March 1, 1876 (see chapter 22 for full report). According to the USLSS Annual Report, "The record of the service for the year 1874–1875 was marked with one memorable shipwreck, that of the Italian bark *Nuova Giovanni*; and it happens that the most single disaster which occurred during the past year also involved the loss of an Italian bark, the *Nuova Ottavia*, which stranded off Currituck Beach, North Carolina, on the night of the 1st of March last, and became a total wreck, whereby nine of her crew were lost, in attempting the rescue of whom the gallant crew of the station also perished. The details of the melancholy disaster are given in the following abstract of the report of the superintendent of the district, dated from the US Life-Saving Station No. 4, Jones Hill, coast of North Carolina."[2]

Barkentine *Samuel Welsh* on February 25, 1888; zero lives lost (could have also been for later Pennys Hill or Poyners Hill).

Schooner *Frank M. McGear* on October 23, 1889; zero lives lost (could have also been for later Pennys Hill or Poyners Hill).

Schooner *Jennie Beasley* on January 26, 1886; zero lives lost.

Schooner *Mattie E. Hiles* on October 30, 1892; zero lives lost.

Partial Wrecks

Brig *William Muir* on April 1, 1871.

Brigantine *Faugh-A-Ballagh* on February 2, 1873.

Bark *Furioso* in March 1874.

Poyners Hill (1878, 1913)

Location: Six and a half miles south of Currituck Lighthouse, Corolla, NC 12. Older station now in Corolla as private home. Built as a result of 1878 *Metropolis* disaster on nearby beach. Second station burned down in early 1970.

Total Wrecks
Schooner *Ada F. Whitney* on September 22, 1885; zero lives lost.
Schooner *Busiris* on October 24, 1889; zero lives lost.
Bark *Vibilia* on May 25, 1891; zero lives lost.

Caffeys Inlet (1874, 1899)

Location: Ten and three-quarter miles south of Currituck Lighthouse, Corolla, NC 12. Once-protected inlet at Dare–Currituck county line. Keeper Malachi Corbell saved two African-American fishermen in June of 1877 and was awarded the Silver Medal. He was the first member of the USLSS to win a Congressional Life-Saving Medal. Now restored as Sanderling Resort Lifesaving Restaurant.

Total Wrecks
Schooner *Henry G. Fay* on April 1, 1876; zero lives lost.
Barkentine *Angela* on March 4, 1883; zero lives lost (see also Paul Gamiels Hill below, also involved).
According to the USLSS Annual Report, "The barkentine *Angela*, of Genoa, Italy, bound with a cargo of iron ore from Cartagena, Spain, to Baltimore, Maryland, and having a crew of 10 men, stranded at midnight 300 yards from shore, and a quarter of a mile south of the Paul Gamiel's [*sic*] Hill Station (6th District), North Carolina. The vessel had sprung a leak, and, being in a sinking condition, was run aground to save the lives of her crew. At the time the sea was high, the surf raging, and the wind blowing freshly from the north. The wreck was immediately seen by the two patrolmen.

"Two shots fired in succession fell short of the wreck, and a third parted the line; a fourth reached the vessel, and the lifesaving crew waited, wondering why the sailors did not haul the line on board. The solution came at daybreak, when the barkentine's men were discovered out at sea in the ship's boat, beyond the line of breakers, having abandoned the vessel under the conviction that she was going to pieces.

"At 9 o'clock, however, the sailors rowed away up the beach, outside the breakers, toward the Caffey's [*sic*] Inlet Station, several miles north of the station at Paul Gamiels Hill. The Caffey's [*sic*] Inlet Station crew then launched their surfboat and after two trips safely landed all 10 of the *Angela*'s crew by 11 a.m. the day after the wreck."[3]

Bark *Harkaway* on November 30, 1885; zero lives lost.

Paul Gamiels Hill (1878, 1909 new site)

Location: Near Duck, five miles north of Kitty Hawk, NC 12. Once located in what is now Seacrest Village. Abandoned by Coast Guard in 1949, used as a private residence, then intentionally burned in early 1960s.

Total Wrecks

Barkentine *Angela* on March 4, 1883; zero lives lost.
Schooner *J. B. Holden* on October 11, 1903; zero lives lost.
Schooner *Charles S. Hirsch* on October 29, 1908; two lives lost.

Kitty Hawk (1874, 1915)

Location: near Mile Post 4½ on Beach Road (Hwy 12); 1874 station now the Black Pelican Oceanfront Restaurant; 1915 station a private home.

Total Wrecks

Schooner *Luola Murchison* on October 3, 1883; zero lives lost.
Schooner *Parrot* on April 7, 1889; two lives lost (could have also been Kill Devil Hills or Nags Head).

Barge *Thomas A. Goddard* on December 9, 1905; zero lives lost.
An excellent example of multiple neighboring stations working together, which quickly became standard operating procedure.

According to the Annual Report: "During a NE gale prevailing on this date a telephone message reached the keeper apprising him of the fact that a steamer had stranded near Kitty Hawk Station and that a barge she had been towing had been cast adrift offshore to prevent it going on the beach. At about the same time the N. and S. patrols reported at the station at Nags Head that they had signed (sighted?) the barge drifting toward the shore, where it appears that she soon brought up. After notifying Kill Devil Hills crew to come down and lend a hand in the work the beach apparatus was quickly transported down the beach.

"Owing to the wreck not remaining stationary, it was with the greatest difficulty that a shot was sent over her . . . The barge now swung completely around, fouling the whip line, her cables parted, and she struck the beach with terrific force, the heavy sea making a clean breech over her. There was no time to be lost . . . the entire crew of 5 men brought safely to shore in the breeches buoy. The destitute men were taken to the station and succored for four days."[4]

So, the wreck was first under the jurisdiction of the Kitty Hawk Station, but then drifted closer to the Nags Head Station, which, in turn, asked the Kill Devil Hills Station to assist.

Kill Devil Hills (1878, 1930s)

Location: Kill Devil Hills. Original station moved in 1986 to Corolla, now restored as Twiddy & Company, real estate and insurance office. Second station a private home located on 1878 site on Beach Road near Mile Post 8½.

Total Wrecks

Schooner *Mary C. Ward* on January 26, 1900; five lives lost (up the Pamlico Sound; could have been Kitty Hawk or Nags Head or no response).

Schooner *Anne Comber* on January 17, 1908; zero lives lost (up the Pamlico Sound; could have been Kitty Hawk or Nags Head or no response).

Schooner *The Josephine* on April 3, 1915; three lives lost.

Nags Head (1874, 1912)

Location: Nags Head. Last station destroyed in 1962 Ash Wednesday storm.

Total Wrecks

Steamer *Ariadne* on February 7, 1873; zero lives lost.

Steamer *Volunteer* on February 23, 1873; zero lives lost.

Steamer *Huron* on November 24, 1877; 103 lives lost (see chapter 19 for full report).

Schooner *Francis E. Waters* on October 24, 1889; six lives lost.

Schooner *George M. Adams* on May 1, 1897; zero lives lost.

Bodie Island (1878, 1923)

Location: Originally, about one mile north of Bodie Island Lighthouse, NC 12. Once called Tommy's Hummock. Old station owned by the National Park Service. Moved south from the dunes to nearby entrance of Bodie Island Lighthouse. NPS use only. The only 1876-style station remaining in North Carolina.

Total Wrecks

Brig *Waltham* on May 4, 1874; zero lives lost.

Schooner *J. Means* on October 12, 1874; zero lives lost.

Schooner *Western Star* on September 11, 1877; zero lives lost.

Schooner *Florence C. Magge* on February 26, 1894; zero lives lost.

Schooner *Laura Nelson* on March 30, 1895; zero lives lost.

Schooner *Milton* on April 27, 1898; zero lives lost.

Schooner *Wm. H. Shubert* on February 16, 1903; zero lives lost.

Schooner *Flora Rogers* on October 23, 1908; zero lives lost.

Partial Wreck

Schooner *Harriet N. Rogers* on January 13, 1873.

Oregon Inlet (1874, 1898)

Location: South bank of Oregon Inlet, Hatteras Island, NC 12. Threatened by erosion. Original station washed away by inlet. Several locations and name changes. A 2008 project raised the station ten feet, replaced floor and roof and reconstructed watchtower. Interior gutted. By 2019, remains abandoned, standing gracefully beside the new $252 million Marc Basnight (formerly Bonner) Bridge.

Total Wrecks

Sloop *June* on August 11, 1899; zero lives lost.

Schooner *J. F. Becker* on April 26, 1903; zero lives lost.

Partial Wreck

Yacht *Black Hawk* on November 6, 1919.

Pea Island (1878, 1881,)1931

Location: Six miles north of Rodanthe village, Hatteras Island, NC 12, two miles north of New Inlet. Now where 2018 NCDOT Captain Richard Etheridge Bridge is located. Formerly located opposite Pea Island National Wildlife Refuge headquarters; remnants of stone foundation at parking area are there. First station destroyed by suspicious fire. 1931 Cookhouse now relocated in Manteo, Collins Park, as a museum.

Total Wrecks

Schooner *M & E Henderson* on November 30, 1879; four lives lost (see chapter 17 for full report).

Schooner *Lizzie S. Haynes* on October 24, 1889; five lives lost.

Schooner *J. W. Gaskill* on February 16, 1891; zero lives lost.

Schooner *E. S. Newman* on October 11, 1896; zero lives lost (see chapter 5 for full report).

Schooner *Montana* on December 11, 1904; one life lost.

Schooner *George N. Reed* on January 20, 1915; zero lives lost.

New Inlet (1882)

Location: About a mile south of Captain Richard Etheridge Bridge, Hatteras Island, NC 12. Destroyed by fire near where inlet cut through Hatteras Island. Never rebuilt.

Total Wrecks

Schooner *Thomas J. Lancaster* on October 5, 1881; seven lives lost.

Schooner *Annie E. Blackman* on October 24, 1889; six lives lost.

Steamer *James Woodall* on January 12, 1896; zero lives lost.

Schooner *John Maxwell* on November 2, 1912; six lives lost.

Chicamacomico (1874, 1911)

Location: Mile Post 39, Hatteras Island, NC 12, Rodanthe. Both stations near original sites in village of Rodanthe. Site of famous 1918 *Mirlo* rescue (see Chapter 3 for full report). Stations are now restored museums.

Total Wrecks

Schooner *William* on February 6, 1873; lives lost unknown.

Schooner *J. H. Lockwood* on November 20, 1876; zero lives lost.

Bark *America* on December 24, 1876; zero lives lost.

Schooner *Iona* on April 9, 1877; lives lost unknown.

Schooner *Benj. W. Robinson* on April 10, 1877; zero lives lost.

Schooner *Florence* on January 5, 1884; zero lives lost.

Bark *Josie Troop* on February 22, 1889; eleven lives lost.

The following is an excerpt from an article published about the *Josie Troop* wreckage.

ELEVEN SEAMEN DROWNED OFF THE NORTH CAROLINA COAST. MARINERS DROWNED.

The Nova Scotian bark *Josie Troop*, with a cargo of chalk and a crew of seventeen men, was wrecked at 7 o'clock last evening at Chicamicomico [*sic*], North Carolina. The master and ten men were drowned. Six were saved. The vessel and cargo are a total loss. The vessel is broken up and strewn on the ocean.

The cause of the disaster was miscalculations owing to thick weather, which made it impossible to get accurate lights and bearings. The crew of Life-Saving Station No. 19 could see no signs of the vessel until the eleven men had been lost and were just in time to save the six survivors. Thus far only one body has come ashore, that of CHARLES MEDEAC.

Pieces of that bulk chalk still wash ashore today.[5]

Schooner *Sue Williams* on March 22, 1890; zero lives lost.

Steamer *Strathairly* on March 24, 1891; nineteen lives lost (see chapter 23 for full report).

Barkentine *Ravenwood* on October 13, 1893; zero lives lost.

Schooner *Samuel W. Tilton* on February 17, 1898; zero lives lost.

Schooner *George L. Fessenden* on April 27, 1898; four lives lost.

Schooner *Minnie Bergen* on August 18, 1899; zero lives lost.

Schooner *Governor Ames* on December 13, 1909; eleven lives lost.

Schooner *Richard F. C. Hartley* on September 2, 1913; two lives lost.

The famous *Mirlo* rescue occurred in 1918 when the station was no longer USLSS, but US Coast Guard. See chapter 3 for full report.

Gull Shoal (1878)

Location: Just south of village of Salvo, near NPS Salvo Day Use Area, Hatteras Island, NC 12. Once called Cedar Hummock, it was destroyed in 1944 hurricane. Where Ramus Midgett saved ten people from wreck of the *Priscilla* in 1899 (see chapter 4 for full report).

Total Wrecks

Schooner *Emma C. Rommell* on January 8, 1884; zero lives lost.

Schooner *Nathaniel Lank* on January 22, 1891; one life lost.

Schooner *Freddie Hencken* on February 26, 1892; zero lives lost.

Barkentine *Henry Norwell* on July 7, 1896; zero lives lost.

Schooner *Alfred Brabrook* on March 7, 1899; zero lives lost.

Schooner *Aaron Reppard* on August 16, 1899; five lives lost (see chapter 10 for full report).

Barkentine *Priscilla* on August 17, 1899; four lives lost (see chapter 4 for full report).

Schooner *Lucy Russell* on June 21, 1903; zero lives lost.

Barge *Saxon* on October 12, 1907; three lives lost.

Schooner *Willie H. Child* on August 17, 1911; zero lives lost.

Schooner *Loring C. Ballard* on April 3, 1915; zero lives lost.

Little Kinnakeet (1874, 1904)

Location: Less than a mile north of village of Avon, Hatteras Island, NC 12, formerly called Kinnakeet. Owned by National Park Service. The 1874 station has been faithfully restored. By 2020, it remains closed to the public.

Total Wrecks

Schooner *Annie E. Pierce* on February 22, 1892; one life lost.

According to the USLSS Annual Report, "On February 22, 1892, the schooner *Annie E. Pierce*, of Somers Point, New Jersey, bound from Bogue Inlet, North Carolina, to New Bedford, Massachusetts, was beached by her master at a point two and one quarter miles south of the Little Kinnakeet Station (6th District), North Carolina, and the death of Alonzo Driscoll, the mate of the vessel, occurred in consequence. As the schooner came into view from seaward through the rain and mist of that stormy February morning, she was espied by a small boy, who called attention to her. At once the keeper saw from the direction she was steering that the vessel would soon be aground, and he made immediate preparations to render assistance. The adjoining stations were spoken [to] by telephone, and in response the keeper and crew of the Gull Shoal Station immediately repaired to the spot indicated, while the keeper of the Big Kinnakeet Station came with horses to assist in hauling the beach cart. In about three-quarters of an hour from the time the vessel was first seen the three life saving [*sic*] crews were upon the beach near the vessel, which had stranded about 150 yards out. Operations began forthwith, under the direction of the keeper of the Little Kinnakeet Station. Communication was soon established, and in less than an hour the entire crew were landed with the beach apparatus, excepting the mate, who had been killed by a heavy sea before the vessel stranded."[6]

Schooner *Nathan Esterbrook Jr.* on February 20, 1893; one life lost.
Schooner *S. G. Hart* on August 10, 1898; zero lives lost.
Schooner *Robert W. Dasey* on August 17, 1899; zero lives lost.
Schooner *Elm City* on March 25, 1912; lives lost unknown.

Big Kinnakeet (1878, 1929)

Location: Around Ramp 38, just south of village of Avon, Hatteras Island, NC 12. Damaged in 1944 hurricane, demolished later. Foundation south of Avon near Askins Creek.

Total Wrecks
Barkentine *Ephraim Williams* on December 22, 1884; zero lives lost (see chapter 11 for full report).
Bark *Wolseley* on April 11, 1899; zero lives lost.

Schooner *Viola W. Burton* on May 27, 1889; zero lives lost.

Schooner *William H. Hopkins* on June 21, 1891; zero lives lost.

Schooner *Martin S. Ebel* on November 5, 1895; zero lives lost.

Schooner *Frances* on February 1, 1910; eight lives lost.

Schooner *Mary S. Eskridge* on December 31, 1911; zero lives lost.

Cape Hatteras (1882)

Location: One mile south of Cape Hatteras Lighthouse near Cape Point, Hatteras Island, NC 12. Early photographs showed them in same photograph. Station and boathouses demolished during early 1930s and replaced by Coast Guard group station in 1935. Protected beaches closest to dangerous Diamond Shoals.

Total Wrecks

Steamer *Enterprise* on December 4, 1882; three lives lost (could also have been later for Ocracoke or Portsmouth).

Schooner *Edna Harwood* on November 31, 1882; one life lost.

Schooner *George S. Marts* on April 16, 1887; two lives lost.

Schooner *Rachel A. Collins* on March 12, 1888; four lives lost.

Schooner *John Shay* on April 17, 1889; six lives lost.

Schooner *Martha* on March 4, 1893; zero lives lost.

Barkentine *J. W. Dresser* on July 23, 1895; zero lives lost.

Steamer *Glanayron* on May 22, 1896; zero lives lost.

Steamer *Hesperides* on October 9, 1897; zero lives lost.

Schooner *William H. Kenzal* on April 5, 1900; lives lost unknown.

Steamer *Virginia* on May 2, 1900; six lives lost.

Schooner *Hettie J. Dorman* on May 5, 1900; zero lives lost.

Steamer *Palestro* on August 9, 1900; zero lives lost.

Schooner *George R. Congdon* on January 31, 1901, zero lives lost.

Steamer *Northeastern* on December 27, 1904; zero lives lost.

Schooner *Cordelia E. Hays* on January 15, 1905; zero lives lost.

Schooner *Robert H. Stevenson* on January 13, 1906; twelve lives lost.

Schooner *Hilda* on February 6, 1907; seven lives lost.

Schooner *Leonora* on January 8, 1908; five lives lost.

Steamer *Brewster* on November 29, 1909; zero lives lost.

Schooner *Harriet C. Kerlin* on February 6, 1911; zero lives lost.

Schooner *Wellfleet* on March 6, 1911; zero lives lost.

Schooner *Harry Prescott* on January 18, 1912; zero lives lost.

Yacht *Idler* on January 14, 1915; twelve lives lost.

Steamer *Prinz Mauritz* on April 3, 1915; forty-nine lives lost.

Creeds Hill (1878, 1918)

Location: Southwest of Frisco village, on Route 12; four miles SW of Cape Hatteras Lighthouse; once located about two miles east of present Hatteras Island site. Now private home.

Total Wrecks

Schooner *Whitney Long* on December 20, 1879; zero lives lost.

Brigantine *Annchen* on July 17, 1888; zero lives lost.

Steamer *Brewster* on November 29, 1909; zero lives lost.

The following letter, written by the *Brewster*'s crew, expresses the sailors' appreciation for the surfmen's efforts.

> SIR: We the undersigned, members of the German steamer *Brewster*, stranded on Diamond Shoals, beg to express our appreciation of the gallant conduct of the crews of the Cape Hatteras, Creeds Hill, and Hatteras Inlet Life-Saving Stations in rescuing us from the above-named vessel on the morning of the 29th of November, 1909, in a very heavy surf, and under exceptional circumstances. We must say that their conduct on this occasion is worthy of the Greatest praise, and the manner in which the rescue was carried out worthy of American seamen. We also thank them for the kindness and hospitality extended to us while at the life-saving stations and assure you that we will never forget same.

F. HINE, *Master*, W. DUHRING, *Chief Engineer*, H.
CLAKSEN, *Second Officer*, O. WALAAS, *Supercargo*[7]

Durants (1878)

Location: Originally called the Hatteras Station. That station was part
of Durant's motel/condo complex near ocean beach in Hatteras Village,
Hatteras Island, NC 12. Totally destroyed when Hurricane Isabel struck
the Outer Banks on September 18, 2003.

Total Wrecks
Schooner *Shiloh* on March 17, 1876; two lives lost.
Schooner *James W. Haig* on September 26, 1882; zero lives lost.
Schooner *James B. Anderson* on January 11, 1889; zero lives lost.
Schooner *Mary A. Trainer* on January 28, 1890; zero lives lost.
Schooner *St. Johns* on March 17, 1890; one life lost.
Schooner *Edward S. Stearns* on March 4, 1895; zero lives lost.
Schooner *J.C. McNaughton* on April 8, 1899; zero lives lost.
Schooner *Clara E. Bergen* on June 26, 1905; zero lives lost.

Hatteras Inlet (1883)

Location: One and a half miles SW of Hatteras Inlet. Earlier location on Hatteras side now destroyed. Later station on Ocracoke Island
destroyed in 1955 storm near where Ocracoke south ferry dock is now
located. Present Coast Guard inlet station near Hatteras ferry docks.

Total Wrecks
Schooner *Clara Davidson* on February 7, 1876; lives lost unknown.
Bark *F. L. Carney* on January 22, 1882; ten lives lost.
Schooner *John N. Parker* on January 8, 1884; zero lives lost.
Schooner *Thomas Sinnickson* on October 12, 1885; zero lives lost.
Schooner *Nellie Wadsworth* on December 6, 1885; zero lives lost.
Schooner *Wesley M. Oler* on December 5, 1902; ten lives lost.

Ocracoke (1905, early 1940s)

Location: Original 1940s station located east of present Coast Guard Station on Silver Lake harbor entrance in Ocracoke village. A gorgeous $7 million restoration in 2011, and now the second of North Carolina's Center for the Advancement of Teaching (NCCAT) facilities.

Total Wrecks

Schooner *E. B. Wharton* on January 31, 1878; lives lost unknown.

Brig *C. C. Overton* on February 1, 1878; lives lost unknown.

Schooner *Eugene* on January 22, 1883; zero lives lost.

Schooner *A. F. Crockett* on February 17, 1885; zero lives lost.

Steamer *Pioneer* on October 12, 1889; zero lives lost.

Schooner *Blanche* on December 17, 1890; zero lives lost.

Schooner *Charles C. Lister Jr.* on January 22, 1891; zero lives lost.

Schooner *Lillie F. Schmidt* on March 9, 1893; zero lives lost.

Schooner *Richard S. Spofford* on December 27, 1894; one life lost.

Schooner *Hester A. Seward* on January 6, 1895; zero lives lost.

Schooner *Addie Henry* on April 14, 1895; zero lives lost.

Schooner *Lizzie S. James* on March 12, 1900; zero lives lost.

Schooner *Ida Lawrence* on December 4, 1902; zero lives lost.

Schooner *George W. Wells* on September 3, 1913; zero lives lost.

Steamer *Ilse of Iona* on December 13, 1914; zero lives lost.

Portsmouth (1894)

Location: Portsmouth village, Portsmouth Island, next island south of Ocracoke Island, now a deserted community owned and maintained by US National Park Service. Station beautifully restored and now open to the public. Coast Guard beach apparatus drill was held there by the Chicamacomico LSS Station Museum for the 2008 Homecoming for the first time since 1937.

Total Wrecks

Schooner *Etta M. Barter* on February 27, 1895; zero lives lost.

Schooner *Sallie Bissell* on March 4, 1895; zero lives lost.

Schooner *S. Warren Hall* on April 5, 1898; zero lives lost.

Schooner *Charmer* on March 4, 1899; zero lives lost.

Schooner *Henrietta Hill* on August 24, 1899; zero lives lost.

Schooner *Three Friends* on February 9, 1900; zero lives lost.

Schooner *Leading Breeze* on November 23, 1901; zero lives lost.

Brigg *Veracruz VII* on May 8, 1903; one life lost.

Schooner *John I. Snow* on January 14, 1907; zero lives lost.

Steamer *Arroyo* on February 20, 1910; zero lives lost.

Core Banks (1896)

Location: Near town of Atlantic, mainland NC, Hwy 12.

Total Wrecks

Schooner *D. D. Haskell* on May 9, 1905; zero lives lost.

Schooner *Melrose* on February 15, 1908; zero lives lost.

Schooner *Thomas G. Smith* on April 10, 1910; zero lives lost.

Cape Lookout (1888)

Location: One and a half miles south of Cape Lookout Lighthouse, Core Banks Island. Crew earned nine Gold Medals for the 1905 rescue of the *Sarah D. J. Rawson*. See chapter 14 for full report.

Total Wrecks

Steamer *Aberlady Bay* on May 10, 1889; zero lives lost.

Schooner *Joseph Rudd* on March 22, 1890; zero lives lost.

Schooner *A. L. & M. Townsend* on July 7, 1891; zero lives lost.

Steamer *Ea* on March 15, 1902; zero lives lost.

Barkentine *Olive Thurlow* on December 5, 1902; one life lost.

Schooner *C. S. Glidden* on March 17, 1903; zero lives lost.

Barkentine *James H. Hamlen* on August 28, 1903; zero lives lost.

Schooner *Joseph W. Brooks* on January 17, 1904; zero lives lost.

Schooner *Kate Spencer* on October 7, 1904; zero lives lost.

Schooner *Sarah D. J. Rawson* on February 9, 1905; one life lost (see chapter 14 for full report).

Schooner *Orient* on April 18, 1908; zero lives lost.

Schooner *Belle O'Neill* on February 3, 1909; zero lives lost.

Schooner *Martha E. Wallace* on December 21, 1910; zero lives lost.

Schooner *Lizzie H. Patrick* on November 27, 1911; zero lives lost.

Steamer *Thistleroy* on December 28, 1911; zero lives lost.

Schooner *Sylvia C. Hall* on March 17, 1915; zero lives lost.

Fort Macon (1904)

Location: Entrance to Beaufort Harbor, north of fort, Beaufort, NC.

Total Wrecks

Sloop *Bronz* on June 21, 1892; zero lives lost (Hatteras Inlet the closest at the time, but very far off; probably no response).

Bogue Inlet (1905)

Location: Inner shore of Bogue Banks, near Swansboro.

Total Wrecks

Schooner *Kate Wentworth* on November 18, 1886; one life lost.

Steamer *Governor Safford* on July 24, 1908; zero lives lost (could have been Core Banks).

Oak Island (1889)

Location: West side of mouth of Cape Fear River, Oak Island, NC.

Total Wrecks

Brig *Wustrow* on August 29, 1893; zero lives lost (see chapter 9).

Schooner *Kate E. Gifford* on August 30, 1893; zero lives lost (see chapter 9).

Schooner *Enchantress* on August 31, 1893; zero lives lost.

Schooner *Mary W. Morris* on October 27, 1893; zero lives lost.

Bark *Ogir* on October 10, 1894; zero lives lost.

Tug *Levi Davis* on November 29, 1896; zero lives lost.

Schooner *William* on January 23, 1898; zero lives lost.

Steamer *Seabright* on September 18, 1901; zero lives lost.

Schooner *Clarence H.* on December 9, 1903; five lives lost.

Cape Fear (1883)

Location: On Smith Island, generally referred to as "Bald Head Island."

Total Wrecks

Steamer *Dos Hermanos* on September 13, 1884; two lives lost (off Cape Fear; could have been Oak Island).

Steamer *Wave* on March 5, 1885; three lives lost (Cape Fear River).

Schooner *Vapor* on November 5, 1885; zero lives lost.

Bark *San Antonio* on January 21, 1890; zero lives lost (Cape Fear River; could have been Oak Island).

Schooner *Hattie S. Clark* on May 15, 1890; five lives lost (could have been Oak Island).

Steam Yacht *Mignon* on September 9, 1890; zero lives lost.

Bark *Casket* on September 13, 1892; zero lives lost (off Frying Pan Shoals; could have been Oak Island).

Bark *Alphild* on February 27, 1893; zero lives lost.

Schooner *Charles C. Dame* on October 14, 1893; zero lives lost.

Schooner *Gertrude* on November 29, 1893; lives lost unknown.

Schooner *Elizabeth A. Baizley* on September 28, 1894; zero lives lost.

Schooner *William H. Allison* on February 3, 1896; zero lives lost.

Schooner *John A. Buttrick* on March 30, 1903; one life lost.

Schooner *Emma C. Middleton* on January 4, 1905; zero lives lost.

Bark *Nineveh* on January 24, 1903; zero lives lost (off Cape Fear; could have been Oak Island).

Schooner *Myrtle Tunnell* on March 9, 1906; zero lives lost.

Schooner *Nellie Floyd* on September 18, 1906; one life lost (off Cape Fear; could have been Oak Island).

Sloop *Harry & Ralph* on June 26, 1907; zero lives lost.

Schooner *Eleazer W. Clark* on November 17, 1909; zero lives lost.

Schooner *Marie Palmer* on November 30, 1909; zero lives lost.

Schooner *James Davidson* on August 26, 1911; zero lives lost.

Schooner *Charles H. Valentine* on August 29, 1911; zero lives lost.

Schooner *Savannah* on December 27, 1912; zero lives lost.

Steamer *Mindora* on January 22, 1915; zero lives lost.

ACKNOWLEDGMENTS

This has been the most enjoyable "work" in my entire highly diverse career; a true labor of love. As with any success, qualified competent teamwork with others was an essential ingredient. Hugely important to this effort was the consistent assistance of my business partner and in-house editor and proofreader—my wife, Linda Molloy. She read every word many times, had numerous great suggestions, and typed most of the manuscript.

My friend, colleague, and inspiring author, Cheryl Shelton Roberts, was immensely helpful. She not only opened the door for me but continued to provide invaluable advice, suggestions, and guidance from her professional experiences.

I am extremely thankful for all of the folks at Globe Pequot, especially my editors, Katie O'Dell, Melissa Hayes, Ellen Urban, and Sarah Parke, for their patient guiding hand throughout, and for Amy Lyons, for accepting my proposal.

All of the graphics were perfected with extensive work by John Havel, who is not only a gifted graphic artist and computer genius, but also my good friend and neighbor.

Finally, a heartfelt thanks to artist Gary Gowans. I had an idea for the book cover and Gary graciously agreed to paint this original artwork, which in a single image captures the essence of the entire book. To anyone who I might have omitted, my grateful thanks to each and all.

Like our honorable and faithful surfmen, we have diligently aimed our "shots" at the facts for 100% accuracy . . . but like them, in spite of strenuous and repeated efforts, a few marks may inadvertently been missed.

APPENDIX A: CHRONOLOGY OF CONSTRUCTION OF NORTH CAROLINA US LIFE-SAVING STATIONS

1874

Jones Hill (renamed Whale Head, then Currituck Beach)

Caffeys Inlet

Kitty Hawk

Nags Head

Bodie Inlet (renamed Oregon Inlet)

Chicamacomico

Little Kinnakeet

1878

Deals Island (renamed Wash Woods)

Old Currituck Inlet (renamed Pennys Hill)

Poyners Hill

Paul Gamiels Hill

Kill Devil Hills

Tommys Hummock (renamed Bodie Island)

Pea Island

Cedar Hummock (renamed Gull Shoal)

Big Kinnakeet

Creeds Hill

Hatteras (renamed Durants)

1880–1905

Cape Hatteras (1880)

New Inlet (1882)

Ocracoke (1883, renamed Hatteras Inlet)
Cape Fear (1883)
Oak Island (1886)
Cape Lookout (1888)
Portsmouth (1894)
Core Banks (1896, renamed Atlantic)
Ocracoke (1904)
Fort Macon (1904)
Bogue Inlet (1905)

APPENDIX B: WHY MORE STATIONS WERE NEEDED

Sites where total wrecks occurred *prior to* station's existence, these all occurred during the period of 1750 to 1915. Partial wrecks at these sites have been omitted.

The "&" designation indicates a new station built to replace older station.

† indicates that this location was quite far away from any station or potential station; location(s) listed are educated guess for probable closest station.

* indicates that some of these locations had another station built at/on the same site after 1915, and so it became a Coast Guard Station.

The purpose here is to demonstrate why USLSS stations were needed in those locations.

Wash Woods (1878)* 7 Total Wrecks
Schooner *Hiram* on January 19, 1837; zero lives lost.
Brig *Ralph* on December 22, 1837; zero lives lost.
Brig *Kilgore* on August 24, 1842; zero lives lost.
Bark *Emilie* on December 3, 1845; seven lives lost.
Schooner *James T. Hatfield* on January 18, 1846; zero lives lost.
Bark *Eliza* on November 28, 1853; one life lost.
Ship *Jane Henderson* on June 21, 1860; zero lives lost.

Pennys Hill (1878) No Total Wrecks

Currituck Beach (1874, 1904) 22 Total Wrecks
Sloop *Betsy* on September 6, 1797; lives lost unknown.
Brig *Georgia* on July 15, 1818; zero lives lost.
Sloop *Revenue* on December day unknown, 1818; zero lives lost.
Sloop *Oran Sherwood* on October 29, 1837; zero lives lost.

Schooner *Wave* on December 9, 1837; zero lives lost.

Schooner *Horse* on January 31, 1838; zero lives lost.

Schooner *American Trader* on August 24, 1841; zero lives lost.

Schooner *Alonzo* on August 24, 1841; zero lives lost.

Schooner *Heroine* on October day unknown, 1841; zero lives lost
(† Whaleshead).

Ship *Victoria* on October 23, 1845; zero lives lost.

Schooner *Evergreen* on January 9, 1849; zero lives lost.

Steamer *Franklin* on September 14, 1850; lives lost unknown.

Schooner *Edward Wood* on November 23, 1850; zero lives lost.

Brig *Mary Turcan* on December 13, 1852; zero lives lost.

Clipper *Rattler* on December 8, 1853; zero lives lost.

Schooner *Baltic* on November day unknown, 1857; lives lost unknown.

Brig *Amanda Coons* on November 11, 1858; lives lost unknown.

Ship *Agamemnon* on March 25, 1859; lives lost unknown.

Federal Steamer *R. B. Forbes* on February 25, 1862; lives lost unknown.

Steamer *Andrew Johnson* on October 5, 1866; lives lost unknown.

Schooner *Martha* on January 10, 1867; zero lives lost.

Bark *M. A. Forbes* on May day unknown, 1870; lives lost unknown.

Poyners Hill (1878, 1913) No Total Wrecks

Caffeys Inlet (1874, 1899) 1 Total Wreck

[Unknown vessel type] *Aid Harrington* on May 23, 1851; zero lives lost.

Paul Gamiels Hill (1878, 1909) No Total Wrecks

Kitty Hawk (1874)* 18 Total Wrecks

Schooner *Emulous* on January 22, 1825; zero lives lost.

Schooner *Diomede* on January 23, 1825; lives lost unknown.

Schooner *Victory* in month and day unknown, 1825; lives lost unknown.

Schooner *Hunter* on August 19, 1837; two lives lost.

Schooner *McDonough* on June 13, 1844; zero lives lost.

Schooner *John Boushell* on January 28, 1851; four lives lost († Albemarle Sound).

Steamer *Mountaineer* on December 25, 1852; zero lives lost.

Schooner *Henrietta Pierce* on January 16, 1853; zero lives lost.

Schooner *Augustus Moore* on April 15, 1853; zero lives lost.

Steamer *Bladen McLaughlin* on May 6, 1853; zero lives lost.

Schooner *Chansfield* on February day unknown, 1860; lives lost unknown († Albemarle Sound).

Confederate Gunboat *Sea Bird* on February 10, 1862; lives lost unknown († Elizabeth City).

Confederate Gunboat *Appomattox* on February 10, 1862; lives lost unknown († Elizabeth City).

Confederate Gunboat *Fanny* on February 10, 1862; lives lost unknown († Elizabeth City).

Confederate Gunboat *Forrest* on February 10, 1862; lives lost unknown († Elizabeth City).

Confederate Gunboat *Black Warrior* on February 10, 1862; lives lost unknown († Elizabeth City).

Federal Gunboat *Southfield* on April 19, 1864; lives lost unknown († Plymouth).

Confederate Ram *Albemarle* on October 27, 1864; lives lost unknown († Plymouth).

Kill Devil Hills (1878) 1 Total Wreck
Ship *William Carlton* on May 15, 1818; zero lives lost.

Nags Head (1874, 1912) 7 Total Wrecks
Unknown vessel in 1778 († Roanoke Inlet). Unknown vessel name, date unknown, lives lost unknown.

Confederate Gunboat *Curlew*, on February 7, 1862 († Roanoke Island).

Pilot Boat *Patriot* on January day unknown, 1813; lives lost unknown.

Brig *Moon* on May 8, 1845; zero lives lost.

Ship *Howell* (or *Howard*) on July 30, 1846; zero lives lost.

Schooner *Antilla* on November 6, 1846; lives lost unknown.

Schooner *Charles* on November day unknown, 1859; lives lost unknown.

Bodie Island (1878)* 14 Total Wrecks
Schooner *Harvest* on November 18, 1825; lives lost unknown.
Schooner *Victory* on February 6, 1837; zero lives lost.
Schooner *Alhambra* on August 26, 1837; zero lives lost.
Brig *Enterprize* on October 9, 1837; one life lost.
Schooner *William J. Watson* on November 15, 1840; zero lives lost.
Schooner *Trident* on June 14, 1842; zero lives lost.
Brig *Marion* on November 4, 1842; two lives lost.
Schooner *Danube* on May 14, 1844; zero lives lost.
Schooner *Rio* in December 1853; zero lives lost.
Steamer *Vera Cruz* in month and day unknown, 1860; lives lost unknown.
Federal Transport *Oriental* on May 8, 1862; lives lost unknown.
Schooner *Adamantine* in November 1867; lives lost unknown.
Bark *Ezra* in September 1869; lives lost unknown.
Steamer *Eagle* on March 4, 1870; zero lives lost.

Oregon Inlet (1874, 1897) 1 Total Wreck
Brig *Quick* in March 1867; five lives lost.

Pea Island (1878, 1881) No Total Wrecks

New Inlet (1882) 8 Total Wrecks
Schooner *Enterprize* on October 27, 1822; zero lives lost.
Steamer *William Gibbons* on October 10, 1836; zero lives lost.
Schooner *C. C. Thorn* on June 2, 1846; lives lost unknown.
Schooner *R. W. Brown* on December 11, 1848; lives lost unknown.
Schooner *Lady Whidbee* on January 17, 1860; zero lives lost.
Brig *Volant* in September 1862; lives lost unknown.
Schooner *Alfred Thomas* on March 10, 1867; lives lost unknown.
Steamer *Flambeau* in March 1867; zero lives lost.

Chicamacomico (1874, 1911) 6 Total Wrecks
Ship *Voucher* on November 19, 1817; zero lives lost.
Packet *Milledgeville* on August 30, 1839; nine lives lost.
Schooner *F. A. Tupper* on March 27, 1843; zero lives lost.
Schooner *P. B. Savery* on August 11, 1851; zero lives lost.
Schooner *Magnolia* on December 3, 1852; one life lost.
Brig *B. T. Martin* on July 24, 1861; lives lost unknown.

Gull Shoal (1878) No Total Wrecks

Little Kinnakeet (1874, 1904) No Total Wrecks

Big Kinnakeet (1878)* No Total Wrecks

Cape Hatteras (1882)* 36 Total Wrecks
Brig *Tyrrel* on July 3, 1759; sixteen lives lost.
Ship *Islington* on March 16, 1820; zero lives lost.
Ship *Congress* on August 24, 1842; seven lives lost.
Schooner *Driver* on January 17, 1844; zero lives lost.
Schooner *Regulus* on January 5, 1846; zero lives lost.
Schooner *Mary Anna* on September 8, 1846; zero lives lost.
Brig *Pennsylvania* on September 24, 1847; zero lives lost.
Schooner *J. P. Bickley* in March 1849; zero lives lost.
Brig *Margaret* on July 24, 1850; zero lives lost.
Brig *Ocean* in July 1850; zero lives lost.
Brig *Belle* in July 1850; zero lives lost.
Schooner *Racer* in July 1850; three lives lost.
Brig *Mary Ellen* in July 1850; zero lives lost.
Steamer *America* on January 30, 1851; zero lives lost.
Schooner *Richard H. Wyatt* on January 31, 1851; zero lives lost.
Schooner *Jane* in June 1851; zero lives lost.
Brig *Albemarle* on September 7, 1853; lives lost unknown.
Schooner *Cassius* on February 12, 1854; zero lives lost.
Bark *Orline St. John* on February 21, 1854; four lives lost.

English ship *Robert Walsh* on March 8, 1854; eleven lives lost.

Bark *Mary Varney* on April 5, 1856; one life lost.

Schooner *A. S. Willers* in September 1857; lives lost unknown.

Confederate Privateer *York* on April 9, 1861; lives lost unknown.

Federal Transport *Governor* on October 31, 1861; lives lost unknown.

Federal Transport *Peerless* on October 31, 1861; lives lost unknown.

Federal Gunboat *Monitor* on December 31, 1862; sixteen lives lost.

Federal Brig *Bainbridge* on August 21, 1863; lives lost unknown.

Brig *Geo. E. Maltby* on January 7, 1867; zero lives lost.

Bark *Istria* in June 1868; twenty-three lives lost.

Steamer *Nevada* on June 4, 1868; one life lost.

Steamer *Thames* on April 6, 1869; lives lost unknown.

Steamer *Key West* in October 1870; zero lives lost.

Schooner *R.B. Thompson* on July 3, 1873; nine lives lost.

Schooner *Spellbourne* in October 1873; zero lives lost.

Schooner *Blaisdell* in May 1875; lives lost unknown.

Wrecking Schooner SS *Lewis* in September 1876; lives lost unknown.

Creeds Hill (1878) 1 Total Wreck*

Schooner *G. W. Carpenter* in April 1867; lives lost unknown.

Durants (1878) No Total Wrecks

Hatteras Inlet (1883) 6 Total Wrecks

Brig *Indus* on December 18, 1837; zero lives lost.

Brig *D. W. Hall* on June 14, 1842; zero lives lost.

Federal Transport *City of New York* on January 15, 1862; lives lost unknown.

Schooner *Vesta* in April 1867; lives lost unknown.

Steamer *Alliance* on March 4, 1869; lives lost unknown.

Steamer *Fairbanks* on December 9, 1870; zero lives lost.

Ocracoke (1905) 14 Total Wrecks*

English ship *Tiger* on June 29, 1585; lives lost unknown.

Gunboat *#140* on September 23, 1814; lives lost unknown.

Sloop *Henry* on December 5, 1819; six lives lost.

Light Ship *Cape Hatteras* in August 1827; two lives lost.

Sloop *Premium* on January 8, 1837; zero lives lost.

Schooner *Aurora* in June 1837; zero lives lost.

Steamer *Home* on October 9, 1837; ninety lives lost (see chapter 12 for full report).

Schooner *Mary* on December 22, 1839; zero lives lost.

Schooner *Lambert Tree* on February 17, 1841; zero lives lost.

Brig *Pioneer* on August 24, 1842; one life lost.

Schooner *Comet* on January 7, 1846; lives lost unknown.

Schooner *Fanny Gray* in March 1849; lives lost unknown.

Brig *Black Squall* on April 8, 1861; lives lost unknown.

Schooner *Daniel Chase* on November 4, 1867; lives lost unknown.

Portsmouth (1894) 3 Total Wrecks

Brigantine *Aurora* on September 19, 1776; zero lives lost.

Federal Gunboat *Pickett* on September 6, 1862; lives lost unknown († Washington).

Federal Gunboat *Underwriter* on February 2, 1864; lives lost unknown († Newbern).

Core Banks or Atlantic (1896) 5 Total Wrecks

Ship *Nuestra de Solidad* on August 18, 1750; († Drum Inlet) zero lives lost.

Schooner *Cumberland* on October 8, 1837; zero lives lost.

Steamer *Pulaski* on June 14, 1838; one hundred lives lost.

Schooner *Mary Bear* on September 9, 1881 (between Core Banks and Cape Lookout); one life lost.

Schooner *Kate Wentworth* on November 18, 1886; one life lost.

Cape Lookout (1888) 11 Total Wrecks

Sloop [Unknown name] in 1666; two lives lost.

Brig *Carroll* on February 8, 1837; zero lives lost.

Schooner *William* on August 29, 1837; lives lost unknown.

Schooner *Argon* in December 1844; zero lives lost.

Schooner *Monterey* on March 7, 1851; zero lives lost.

Steamer *Oneota* in November 1867; lives lost unknown.

Steamer *Patapsco* on September 12, 1868; zero lives lost.

Steamer *Gulf City* on June 11, 1869; twenty-two lives lost.

Steamer *La Republique* in February 1871; zero lives lost.

Ship *Pontiac* in February 1871; lives lost unknown.

Schooner *Crissie Wright* on January 11, 1886; six lives lost.

Fort Macon (1904) 5 Total Wrecks

Schooner *Seaman* on March 5, 1837; zero lives lost († New River Inlet).

Steamer *Pulaski* on June 14, 1938; one hundred lives lost († off New River).

Schooner *Walter J. Doyle* in March 1852; lives lost unknown († Beaufort Bar).

Schooner *Sun* on January 13, 1854; lives lost unknown († Beaufort Inlet).

Blockade Runner *Nutfield* on February 4, 1864; lives lost unknown († New River Inlet).

Bogue Inlet Swansboro (1905) 4 Total Wrecks

Vessel type unknown *El Salvador* on August 18, 1750; lives lost unknown († Topsail Inlet).

Steamer *Sam Berry* on January 12, 1856; one life lost († Masonboro Inlet).

Federal Gunboat *Columbia* on January 14, 1863; lives lost unknown († Masonboro Inlet).

Blockade Runner *Pevensey* on June 9, 1864, lives lost unknown.

Oak Island (1889) 6 Total Wrecks

Blockade Runner *Elizabeth* on September 24, 1863; lives lost unknown († Lockwoods Folly).

Blockade Runner *Bendigo* on January 4, 1864; lives lost unknown
(† Lockwoods Folly).

Blockade Runner *Vesta* on January 10, 1864; lives lost unknown
(† Tubbs Inlet).

Federal Gunboat *Iron Age* on January 11, 1864; lives lost unknown
(† Lockwoods Folly).

Blockade Runner *Ranger* on January 11, 1864; lives lost unknown
(† Lockwoods Folly).

Schooner *Mary J. Fisher* on August 24, 1881; four lives lost (south of
Oak Island).

Cape Fear (1883) 40 Total Wrecks

Brigantine [Unknown] in June 1526; lives lost unknown.

Flyboat [Unknown] in 1665; zero lives lost.

Brig *Escambia* on March 25, 1840; lives lost unknown (Frying Pan
Shoals).

Ship *Flora* on March 28, 1840; lives lost unknown (Frying Pan Shoals).

Brig *Ashley* on June 2, 1842; zero lives lost.

Brig *Rodney* on June 20, 1848; zero lives lost.

Blockade Runner *Modern Greece* on June 27, 1862; lives lost unknown.

Confederate Light Ship *Frying Pan Shoals* on December 31, 1862; lives
lost unknown († Cape Fear River).

Blockade Runner *Golden Liner* on April 27, 1863; lives lost unknown
(† Cape Fear River).

Blockade Runner *Kate (2nd)* on July 12, 1863; lives lost unknown
(† Smiths Island).

Blockade Runner *Hebe* on August 18, 1863; lives lost unknown († near
Cape Fear).

Blockade Runner *Alexander Cooper* on August 22, 1863; lives lost
unknown († near Cape Fear).

Blockade Runner *Arabian* on September 15, 1863; lives lost unknown
(† near Cape Fear).

Blockade Runner *Phantom* on September 23, 1863; lives lost unknown
(† Rich Inlet).

Blockade Runner *Douro* on October 11, 1863; lives lost unknown (†
Wrightsville).

Blockade Runner *Venus* on October 21, 1863; lives lost unknown (†
near Cape Fear).

Blockade Runner *Beauregard* on December 11, 1863; lives lost
unknown († Carolina Beach).

Blockade Runner *Antonica* on December 19, 1863; lives lost unknown
(Frying Pan Shoals).

Blockade Runner *Dee* on February 6, 1864; lives lost unknown († near
Cape Fear).

Blockade Runner *Wild Dayrell* on February 1, 1864; lives lost unknown
(† Stump Inlet).

Blockade Runner *Fanny & Jenny* on February 9, 1864; lives lost
unknown († Wrightsville).

Blockade Runner *Emily of London* on February 9, 1864; lives lost
unknown († Wrightsville).

Blockade Runner *Spunkie* on February 9, 1864; lives lost unknown (†
near Cape Fear).

Confederate Gunboat *Raleigh* on May 7, 1864; lives lost unknown (†
Cape Fear River).

Blockade Runner *Georgiana McCaw* on June 2, 1864; lives lost
unknown.

Blockade Runner *Florie* on September 10, 1864; lives lost unknown (†
Cape Fear bar).

Blockade Runner *Badger* on September 10, 1864; lives lost unknown (†
Cape Fear bar).

Confederate Gunboat *North Carolina* in September 1864; lives lost
unknown († Cape Fear River).

Blockade Runner *Condor* on October 1, 1864; lives lost unknown (†
near Cape Fear).

Blockade Runner *Ella* on December 3, 1864; lives lost unknown.

Federal Gunboat *Louisiana* on December 24, 1864; lives lost unknown
(† Fort Fisher).

Confederate Gunboat *Tallahassee* on January 15, 1865; lives lost unknown († near Cape Fear).

Blockade Runner *Cape Fear* in January 1865; lives lost unknown († Cape Fear River).

Blockade Runner *North Heath* in January 1865; lives lost unknown († Cape Fear River).

Steamer *Francis* on December 30, 1867; zero lives lost († Carolina Beach).

Schooner *Eleanor T.* on February 4, 1870; five lives lost († Carolina Beach).

Schooner *Electric* on August 21, 1876; zero lives lost (between Cape Fear and Oak Island).

Schooner *Minnie* on April 12, 1882; zero lives lost.

Schooner *Mercy T. Trundy* on April 24, 1882; zero lives lost.

Schooner *Robbie L. Foster* on October 14, 1882; zero lives lost.

ENDNOTES

Chapter 1

1 *Lifeboat Magazine Archive*, 1880. *Lifeboat* magazine is published quarterly and mailed to RNLI members around the UK and Ireland.

2 *Regulations for the Government of the Life-Saving Service of the United States*, 1899, Washington, DC: Government Printing Office, table of contents.

3 Superintendent Sumner I. Kimball's 1894 publication, *Organization and Methods of the United States Life-Saving Service*, Treasury Department, Life-Saving Service, Office of the General Superintendent, Washington, DC, January 5, 1894.

4 Ibid.

5 Ralph Shanks, *The US Life-Saving Service: Heroes, Rescues, and Architecture of the Early Coast Guard*, Novato, CA: Costano Books, 1996, p. 1.

Chapter 2

1 David Stick, *Graveyard of the Atlantic: Shipwrecks of the North Carolina Coast*, Chapel Hill: University of North Carolina Press, 1952.

2 Nell Wise Wechter, *Taffy of Torpedo Junction*, Chapel Hill: University of North Carolina Press, 1996.

Chapter 3

1 Ray McAllister, *Hatteras Island: Keeper of the Outer Banks*, Google Books, 2009. Award-winning coastal writer Ray McAllister returns to the site of his family's annual vacations a quarter-century ago. Much has changed on Hatteras. But even more has not. Hatteras has kept its soul.

Chapter 6

1 Stick, *Graveyard of the Atlantic*, p. 222.

2 *Outer Banks Sentinel*, April 22, 2006.

Chapter 7

1 Coast Guard Compass Blog, "Shipmate of the Week: Rescuers of the HMS *Bounty*, Lt. Stephanie Young, November 2, 2012. The official blog of the US Coast Guard, found at https://compass.coastguard.blog.

2 Ibid.

3 Ibid.

4 The Weather Channel Special, *Coast Guard: HMS* Bounty *Rescue*, Al Roker Productions, November 26, 2012.

5 Ibid.

6 National Transportation Safety Board, Marine Accident Brief MAB-14-03. Adopted: February 6, 2014. www.ntsb.gov/investigations/acci dentreports/pages/mab1403.aspx.

7 "Coast Guard Blames Management, Captain for Sinking of HMS *Bounty*," by Thom Patterson, CNN, June 13, 2014.

Chapter 8

1 *The Telegraph*, December 6, 2008, www.telegraph.co.uk.

2 Ibid.

3 Mike Daniel of Intersal, Inc., news conference, March 3, 1997.

4 "Blackbeard's Ship Confirmed off North Carolina: Wreck's Large Size, Weapons that of 18th-Century Pirate, Experts Say," by Willie Drye, for *National Geographic* News, August 29, 2011.

5 QAR Conservation Lab, www.qaronline.org/conservation/queen -annes-revenge-lab. From QAR@ncdcr website, "On November 21, 1996, a search team from the private research firm Intersal, Inc., operat-ing under a permit from the N.C. Department of Natural and Cultural Resources found a cluster of cannon and anchors on the seabed near historic Beaufort Inlet."

Chapter 9

1 Public Records, Brunswick County Government, www.brunswick countync.gov/info/public-records.

2 HurricaneScience.org.

Chapter 10

1 *Annual Report of the Operations of the United States Life-Saving Service* for the fiscal year ending June 30, 1900, p. 21.

2 Ibid.

Chapter 11

1 Origin of Keeper Patrick Etheridge's remark, "The Blue Books says . . . ," from the Coast Guard Historian's Office, a letter to the editor of the old *Coast Guard Magazine* written by CBM Clarence P. Brady, USCG (Ret.) which was published in the March 1954 issue, p. 2.

2 *Regulations, LSS,* 1899, Article VI, "Action at Wrecks," section 252, p. 58.

Chapter 12

1 Stick, *Graveyard of the Atlantic*, p. 24.

Chapter 13

1 Amadas and Barlowe Report, The Dempsey Archives, www .thedempseyarchives.com/1585.htm.

2 Lee Miller, *Roanoke: Solving the Mystery of the Lost Colony*, New York: Penguin Books, 2000, p. 86. © page lists: New York, London, Australia, Toronto, New Delhi, New Zealand and Johannesburg.

3 Paul Hulton, *America 1585: The Complete Drawings of John White*, Chapel Hill: University of North Carolina Press and British Museum Publications, 1984, p. 5.

4 Ibid., p. 23.

Chapter 14

1 *Annual Report, USLSS,* for the fiscal year ending June 30, 1905, p. 38.

2 Ibid., p. 38.

3 Ibid., p. 39.

Chapter 15

1 Tom Crouch, *The Bishop's Boys: A Life of Wilbur and Orville Wright*, New York and London: W. W. Norton & Co., 1989, p. 218, in a speech in Chicago to the Western Society of Engineers, 1901.

Chapter 16

1 "The Legend of the Ghost Ship: *Carroll A. Deering*," National Park Foundation, www.nationalparks.org/connect/blog/legend-ghost-ship-carroll-deering.

2 "The *Carroll A. Deering*," The Mysterious Miscellany, https://themysteriousmiscellany.wordpress.com/2017/04/10/carroll-a-deering.

3 "The Mystery of the *Carroll A. Deering* Shipwreck," Carolina Designs, https://blog.carolinadesigns.com/2018/04/20/the-mystery-of-the-carrol-a-deering-shipwreck.

4 "*Carroll A. Deering*'s Vanished Crew," Historic Mysteries, www.historicmysteries.com/carroll-a-deering.

5 Ian Harvey, article for *The Vintage News*, January 5, 2018.

6 Bland Simpson, *Ghost Ship of Diamond Shoals: The Mystery of the Carroll A. Deering*, Chapel Hill: University of North Carolina Press, 2002, p. 79.

7 Ibid., p. 228.

Chapter 17

1 *Annual Report, USLSS*, for the fiscal year ending 1880, p. 19.

2 Ibid., p. 19.

3 Ibid., p 20.

Chapter 18

1 Gordon Kelly, "*Titanic* Anniversary: The Myth of the Unsinkable Ship," *BBC Future*, April 20, 2012.

2 Catherine Kozak, "Titanic's Chilling NC Connection," *Coastal Review Online*, April 1, 2013.

3 Ibid.

Chapter 19

1 Stick, *Graveyard of the Atlantic*, p. 78.

2 Joe Mobley, *Ship Ashore! The US Lifesavers of Coastal North Carolina*, Office of Archives and History, Raleigh: North Carolina Department of Cultural Resources, 1994, p. 57.

3 Stick, *Graveyard of the Atlantic*, p. 103.

Chapter 20

1 Diana Sherbs, "A Little Piece of Kimball's Legacy of Standardization," *Coast Guard Compass Archive*, April 25, 2018.

2 Dr. Dennis Noble.

3 Stick, *Graveyard of the Atlantic*, p. 92.

4 Ibid., p. 95.

5 Bill Sharpe, *The State*, November 3, 1951.

6 Stick, *Graveyard of the Atlantic*, p. 98.

7 Ibid., p. 98.

8 Sharpe, *The State*, November 3, 1951.

Chapter 21

1 Barbara Glakas, *Herndon Patch* feature of Herndon Historical Society, "Remembering Herndon's History: The SS *George Law*: The Life and Death of the Ship that Became the SS *Central America*," www .herndonhistoricalsociety.org.

2 Barbara Glakas, *Hidden History of Herndon*, Charleston, SC: The History Press, 2019.

3 H. H. Childs, "Loss of the *Central America*: Further Particulars of the Disaster," *Milwaukee Daily Sentinel*, September 22, 1857.

4 Ibid.

5 Mike Fuljenz, "The Association of Mature American Citizens," *The AMAC Magazine*, April 5, 2018.

6 Sean Munger, "The SS *Central America*: The Ship that Helped Wreck a Nation," September 12, 2013, https://seanmunger.com/category/history-is-cool.

7 Andrew Marszal, "What Was the SS *Central America*—or 'Ship of Gold'—and Why Did It Sink?" *UK Daily Telegraph*, January 29, 2015.

Chapter 22

1 Stick, *Graveyard of the Atlantic*, p. 71.

2 *Annual Report, USLSS*, for the fiscal year ending June 30, 1876, p. 12.

3 Stick, *Graveyard of the Atlantic*, p. 72.

4 *Annual Report, USLSS*, for the fiscal year ending June 30, 1876, pp. 12–13.

5 Joe Mobley, *Ship Ashore! The US Lifesavers of Coastal North Carolina*, Office of Archives and History, North Carolina Department of Cultural Resources, Raleigh, 1994, p. 51.

6 *Annual Report, USLSS*, for the fiscal year ending June 30, 1876, p. 14.

Chapter 23

1 Stick, *Graveyard of the Atlantic*, p. 125.

2 Definition of "tramp steamer," *Encyclopaedia Britannica*, July 20, 1998.

Conclusion

1 *Annual Report, USLSS*, for the fiscal year ending June 30, 1909, p. 121.

2 *Annual Report, USLSS*, for the fiscal year ending June 30, 1876, p. 11 (first paragraph).

3 *Annual Report, USLSS*, for the fiscal year ending June 30, 1883, p. 207.

4 *Annual Report, USLSS,* for the fiscal year ending June 30, 1906, p. 113.

5 "Eleven Seamen Drowned Off the North Carolina Coast; Mariners Drowned," *Sunday Inter Ocean*, Chicago, Illinois, February 24, 1889.

6 *Annual Report, USLSS,* for the fiscal year ending June 30, 1892, p. 39 (first paragraph).

7 *Annual Report, USLSS,* for the fiscal year ending June 30, 1910, p. 116.

INDEX

ABOUT THE AUTHOR

James D. Charlet is an authority on the US Life-Saving Service on North Carolina's iconic Outer Banks and contributes to local and national media with articles on Outer Banks and nautical history. James taught North Carolina history for twenty-four years and authored a state-adopted textbook on the subject. He has worked with the Wright Brothers National Memorial, the Cape Hatteras Lighthouse, Fort Raleigh National Historic Site, was Lead Interpreter at Roanoke Island Festival Park (celebrating the Roanoke Voyages), and—most importantly—has been involved with the Chicamacomico Life-Saving Station Historic Site & Museum for twenty-one years and was the site manager of the Historic Site for ten years, retiring from there in 2015. In his spare time, James conducts tours, educational programs, and speaking engagements and live presentations as "Keeper James."